# The Poetics of Romanticism

**Sketch of John Keats (1816)**
by Benjamin Robert Haydon
National Portrait Gallery, London

# The Poetics of Romanticism
*toward a reading of John Keats* | M.A.Goldberg

THE ANTIOCH PRESS YELLOW SPRINGS OHIO 1969

Designed by David Battle.
Copyright 1969
by M. A. Goldberg.
All rights reserved.
Library of Congress
Catalog Card No. 68–31035.
Printed in the United States of America.

For Hannah

**List of Illustrations**  (following page 88)

. . . For the publication of the *Letters to Fanny Brawne* I can see no good reason whatever. Their publication appears to me, I confess, inexcusable; they ought never to have been published. But published they are, and we have to take notice of them. . . . [They reveal] relaxed self-abandonment something under-bred and ignoble, as of a youth ill brought up, without the training which teaches us that we must put some constraint upon our feelings and upon the expression of them.

—Matthew Arnold

The Letters [of Keats] are certainly the most notable and most important ever written by any English poet. . . . There is hardly one statement of Keats about poetry, which, when considered carefully and with due allowance for the difficulties of communication, will not be found to be true; and what is more, true for greater and more mature poetry than anything that Keats ever wrote.

—T. S. Eliot

# Directions and Indirections

To any examination of a major writer like John Keats, the critical reader must bring an enormous sensitivity and an immensity of erudition. Unfortunately, all too few of us possess this critical apparatus.

Analysis alone will simply not do. The techniques of modern criticism appear all the more limited in approaching the romantics, whose poetics were antithetical to dissective analysis. "The Genius of Poetry . . . cannot be matured by law & precept, but by sensation & watchfulness in itself—That which is creative must create itself," Keats was to explain, just as in *Lamia* he was to point out that men who would "conquer all mysteries by rule and line" are fated to "unweave a rainbow." *Ltr. to Hessey,* *8 Oct. 1818*

This same antithesis, between precepts and sensations, between dissective analysis and creative beauty, was developed by most of the romantics. Shelley had distinguished between two classes of mental action—reason and imagination—and defined poetry as "the expression of the imagination." The distinction was basic to Wordsworth and Coleridge, as well as to Blake. It would seem as if sensitivity to romantic poetry almost precludes sympathy with structural analysis. The methods and aims of

modern criticism, all too frequently starting and ending with structural analyses, appear to preclude any sympathy with the anti-rational, anti-conceptualizing romantics.

And yet, much is to be said for the methods of modern criticism. Rational, conceptual, intellectual, analytic, modern methods have paradoxically been most instrumental in pointing up the subtle beauties and the structural complexities of Keats's poetry. They have done this, despite Keats's insistence that his poems "will explain themselves—as all poems should do without any comment." Modern criticism has also been eminently successful in turning readers toward the poetic text itself, diverting them from vague and impressionistic statements about Keats's poetry, from a search for sources and analogues, from the tempting surrogates offered by biography or history or philosophy. At one time, it was relatively simple to subordinate poetry to these peripheral concerns.

*Ltr. to George &*
*Georgiana,*
*2 Jan. 1819*

In this examination of Keats's poetics, I cannot dismiss the letters—those remarkable letters he wrote to his friends and family—as a peripheral concern. Throughout, my primary concern is with the Keatsian poetics, and those letters reveal so much about the artistry, about the creative process of Keats. They do this with a profundity that is only implicit—as well it ought to be!—within the poems themselves.

Through the letters, the poetry assumes a larger dimension. What Keats was trying to do is even more illuminated by examining both the poetry and the letters within the larger context of his age. After all, Keats was trying to work through problems not too far removed from those with which his contemporaries were concerned. Despite their differences, some quite large, poets in early nineteenth-century England tended to share similar assumptions and reflect similar attitudes—what we still call, despite admonitions to the contrary, "romanticism." To see with some clarity what Keats was doing, we must recognize what he was *not* doing, but what his contemporaries *were* doing with their "romanticisms." Keats was writing more like Wordsworth than Pope. Yet he was not writing Wordsworthian verse, and his good poetry is immediately distinguishable from that of Shelley or Byron or Felicia Hemans. Even when he was at times deliberately imitating Spenser or

Shakespeare or Milton, the voice is immediately recognizable.

The search for clarity takes the critic in ever-widening circles. Recognizing what the romantics were about makes it essential to understand what they were not about—those attitudes and assumptions common to the eighteenth-century syndrome against which Keats and his contemporaries were presumably revolting. Many of the errors that have crept into our thinking about the romantics emerge, I suspect, from their own persistence in viewing their movement as a revolution against neo-classical standards. Still, how is it possible to comprehend English neo-Augustan classicism without seeing its counterpart in France? or without grappling with earlier classical motifs—in ancient Greece and Rome? in the medieval tendency to subvert classicism to the more primary interests of Christianity? in that revival of classical learning which we call the Renaissance?

Ultimately, criticism may be an art; but initially, it is a problem of epistemology. Having begun with a simple enough inquiry—what can he know about a particular sonnet or ode by Keats?—the critic is almost invariably limited by his own knowledge into drawing arbitrary lines and artificial boundaries. Yet, whatever most illuminates the art demands to be admitted. The whole of Western culture prior to Keats has been invested in the man; surely, nothing less should be admitted for the art. Thus, Keats's knowledge of Horace or Boileau may have been second-hand and superficial; his reading of Plato may have been cursory; his grasp of mythology may have been restricted to Sandys' translation of Ovid, Tooke's *Pantheon,* and Lemprière's *Classical Dictionary;* he was probably totally ignorant of works by Alexander Ross or Julius Caesar Scaliger to which I later allude. But Horace was part of the tradition which Keats inherited; so were Boileau and Ross.

The problem is vast. But this is not the whole of it. The modern reader must gravitate between two poles, between the realities of Keats and the realities of his own critical self. There is the Keatsian, early nineteenth-century vision to apprehend, the whole of what is encompassed by that vision. There is also the critic's mid-twentieth-century vision, one which necessarily colors any perspective of art emanating out of an earlier era.

To lose sight of either is to abandon self to the vagaries of the moment, to subordinate art to the egotism of self, to confuse clarity of vision with personal tastes. The problems of criticism are immense—perhaps even insuperable, for the realities of any writer are inextricably bound up with his language—his vocabulary, his rhythms, his intonations, his imagery; and with Keats, perhaps even the curious punctuation and spelling. Recognizing this, I have tried to capture that language when writing of the Keatsian poetic and to rely upon Keats himself, whenever possible, to do much of the speaking. The marginal notes are aimed at identifying the Keatsian source, when this is not apparent from the text, without disrupting the textual flow.

Like any literary movement, the romantics represent a rather sprawling and diffused entity. The characteristics of the movement are somewhat evasive, although handbooks, encyclopedias, dictionaries, and some literary critics spell out these characteristics with much clarity. Like a Keatsian ode, however, the romantic movement cannot be packaged into a brief paraphrase, a catalog of properties, or a succinct analysis of patterns. At best, one hopes to speak about the constant elements, the inner correspondences of a poetic movement, in order to emerge with some larger understanding of the complexities involved.

Some larger understanding can emerge if one of the major misconceptions about the romantics can be broken down. I refer here to the notion that romanticism and classicism are antithetical and mutually exclusive. Romanticism, I would suggest, is but another way of looking upon and using classical standards—the classicism of Sophocles and Phidias, Socrates and Plato. John Keats, assuming the materials and ends of classicism, interpreted these according to his own particular values. Of course Keats has more in common with Shelley than with Socrates. What they have in common, I would insist, is a particular variant of classicism. By and large, the romantic writers of the early nineteenth century developed a common approach to classicism—much as Sophocles shares in the classicism of Plato and Aristotle, and Pope in the classicism of Boileau and Swift.

Of late, we have come to interpret history in a different way, as a force within us, rather than behind us. Despite the anti-romanticism of the last half-century, we have come increasingly to recognize that the early decades of the nineteenth century lie within us still. We can no more erase romanticism from our being than we can eliminate the Bible, Socrates—or our own childhood. These all lie too deeply imbedded. They have gone too much into our making for us to do more than repress them. We may not choose to look at them; or we may learn to develop new attitudes toward them. But we cannot make them go away.

With Keats, the critical question is inevitably colored or discolored to begin with, by our own attitudes toward romanticism. How Keats was writing poetry is simply an extension of the question confronting him of how poetry should be written. The reader today is confronted with a permutation of that same problem: how poetry ought to be written now, or always; by Keats, or by ourselves.

Although the critic's task is immense, a step in the direction of clarity, however hesitant, is essential. This is preferable, it seems to me, to standing with both feet firmly planted upon familiar, non-controversial, but insignificant grounds. Keats might have been of the same opinion, recognizing that "in Endymion, I leaped headlong into the Sea, and thereby have become better acquainted with the Soundings, the quicksands, & the rocks, than if I had stayed upon the green shore." Far better to wrestle with dragons and lose, than to wrestle with gnats and win. *Ltr. to Hessey, 8 Oct. 1818*

Keats himself is a dragon of sorts, despite his youth, his relatively small production, the tentative and experimental attitude he maintained toward his own work. Like Shakespeare, he could pit himself against the jejune and the significant, against the trivial and the overwhelming. He seemed capable of absorbing everything. I do not mean to suggest in this comparison of Keats with Shakespeare—or in later comparisons with Socrates and Dostoevsky, Zola and Joyce—that these dragons are of equal stature. I mean rather that in the process of achieving some perspective toward Keats—toward the few really good poems, the many insightful and fragmented letters

—the whole of literary history must be brought to bear. This is what is so impossible, and yet so necessary, about the critic's

*Ltr. to Reynolds,*
*3 Feb. 1818*

task. "Why should we be owls, when we can be Eagles?" Keats himself was to ask.

My main intention throughout this volume is not to examine the whole or even part of Keats's poetry, as such, but to see the extent to which Keats's many observations about poetry and the poetic process can be understood as a relatively coherent whole, rather than as a series of highly illuminating but uncoordinated fragments. Since my concern is primarily with his poetic theory as an insight into romantic poetics, Keats's verse is examined only insofar as it illuminates that theory.

Accordingly, the central chapters aim at developing the poetics of Keats as revealed in theory and practice: the particular objects and events which the creative poet had at his disposal before their transformation into an artistic form (Chapters 5 and 6); the procedure by which these materials were transformed through the poetic consciousness during the creative process (Chapters 7 and 8); the manner of artistic representation—the particular craft by which materials, pursued through the consciousness of the artist, were to be translated into an art form (Chapters 9 through 11). In speaking of art as representational, I am not limiting myself to the idea of naturalistic or photographic representation. I recognize that Keatsian poetry—no less than Cubism or Greek tragedy, Surrealism or the sculpture of Michelangelo, Abstract Expressionism or the comedies of Shakespeare—can be mimetic of the instinctive, the irrational, the imaginative.

Those central chapters of Book Two, "The Keatsian Poetic," aim at illuminating the poetic theory and practice of Keats. The poet is examined alongside his English contemporaries—Wordsworth, Blake, Shelley, Hazlitt and Haydon—but he is also viewed within the tradition he inherited, the classicism of ancient Greece as it developed through the eighteenth century; and within that tradition as it developed after Keats, with Zola and Dostoevsky, Conrad, Joyce, Kafka, and Sartre.

Book One, "The Keatsian Inheritance," explores the earlier tradition of artistic and poetic theory, and the departure of romantic aesthetics from that inheritance. Like the late phase

of Greco-Roman art, and like those revivals of classicism which we call the Renaissance or the Age of Reason, the romantic movement of the early nineteenth century is not necessarily a decline from or a perversion of classicism. It offers another mood of classicism, perhaps even an up-dating of the values of Periclean Athens.

Book Three, "The Keatsian Aftermath," traces through the twentieth-century development. In some sense, modern writers —Proust and Joyce, Yeats and Dylan Thomas and T. S. Eliot —are all extensions of that classical tradition, as it developed through the romantics.

One major conclusion, as it emerges from that final book, is that modern poetry and criticism—and indeed, modern art in general—ought properly to turn to Keats and to the romantics for a better sense of direction. It has been almost a half century since T. S. Eliot directed our attention to the seventeenth-century metaphysicals and instituted, almost single-handedly, a revolution in our ways of thinking with and about poetry. We are now, I would contend, sufficiently removed from the romantics, thanks to Mr. Eliot, to have a good look at what they were trying to do. We cannot, as Eliot himself came to recognize, ignore a century and a half within the mainstream of English poetry and criticism, particularly when we seem now to be entering into a new current of that mainstream, a neo-romanticism with perceptible debts to Keats and to that earlier phase.

---
Book One
---

# The Keatsian
# ❧Inheritance❧

By magic songs
and incantations,
even the moon
can be dragged down
from the heavens.
—Virgil, *Eclogue VIII*

# 1
# John Keats and the Elgin Marbles

Always the victim of intensities far more enthralling than he could himself endure, John Keats seems to have begun a close friendship with the painter Benjamin Robert Haydon almost immediately after they were introduced in the late autumn of 1816. Keats was twenty-one. He had just become eligible to practice as apothecary-physician, following a long apprenticeship to Thomas Hammond, surgeon at Edmonton, and a year's residence at Guy's Hospital. But already his brain was teeming with the possibilities for a poetic career. That spring, his first published poem, the sonnet *O Solitude,* had appeared in *The Examiner,* and he was receiving mixed praise on some of his other verse.

Within three years, by September of 1818, a disenchantment set in, as Keats awakened with some bitterness to the arrogance and egotism of Haydon. But until then, his letters to Haydon and about him were charged with a devotion that verged on idolatry. Keats was delighted to meet "this glorious Haydon and all his Creation." He became attached to the painter with an extravagant affection which Haydon seemed to reciprocate, and before many meetings Keats was addressing a sonnet to him.

*Ltr. to Clarke, 31 Oct. 1816*

*Ltr. to Haydon, 20 Nov. 1816*

Haydon was himself fascinated by the precocity of Keats's poetical and intellectual powers. In his *Autobiography* he records that he liked the younger man so much that he immediately issued a general invitation. Before long, they were on intimate terms. Keats was to visit his painting-room at any hour of the day or night, and he was welcome at all times. At their first meeting Haydon was almost thirty-one. He was already an established painter, a friend of some of the leading critics and poets. His judgment of the Elgin Marbles had just been vindicated, for after an eight-year controversy in which he had been most effusive and effective, the British government had finally agreed to purchase from Lord Elgin these marble ruins from the Parthenon and to deposit them for the nation in the British Museum.

Haydon had first seen the Marbles in 1808, when they were still ranged in a damp and dirty penthouse in Park Lane. Their effect upon him was electrifying. Instantaneously, the future of his own painting and of art itself seemed stretched before him in these slabs from out of the distant past:

The first thing I fixed my eyes on was the wrist of a figure in one of the female groups, in which were visible, though in a feminine form, the radius and ulna. I was astonished, for I had never seen them hinted at in any female wrist in the antique. I darted my eye at the elbow, and saw the outer condyle visibly affecting the shape as in nature. I saw that the arm was in repose and the soft parts in relaxation. That combination of nature and idea which I had felt was so much wanting for high art was here displayed to midday conviction. My heart beat! . . .

I felt the future, I foretold that they would prove themselves the finest things on earth, that they would overturn the false beau-ideal, where nature was nothing, and would establish the true beau-ideal, of which nature alone is the basis.

I shall never forget the horses' heads—the feet in the metopes! I felt as if a divine truth had blazed inwardly upon my mind and I knew that they would at last rouse the art of Europe from its slumber in the darkness.

I do not say this *now*, when all the world acknowledges it, but I said it then, *when no one would believe me*. I went home in perfect excitement, Wilkie trying to moderate my enthusiasm with his national caution.

. . . I passed the evening in a mixture of torture and hope; all night I dozed and dreamed of the marbles. I rose at five in a fever of excitement, tried to sketch the Theseus from memory, did so, and saw that I comprehended it.

His "fever" spread. Eight years later, shortly after their initial meeting, the infection was passed to Keats.

*Endymion,* Keats's first major venture with a classical theme, was still in fermentation early in March of 1817, when the young poet was induced by Haydon to share with him his experience with the Greek Marbles. Keats was equally intoxicated. Overwhelmed by this new kind of beauty, he sat down at once to write two sonnets. The first, *On Seeing the Elgin Marbles,* gravitated about his own experience:

> My spirit is too weak—mortality
>     Weighs heavily on me like unwilling sleep,
>     And each imagin'd pinnacle and steep
> Of godlike hardship tells me I must die
> Like a sick Eagle looking at the sky.
>     Yet 'tis a gentle luxury to weep
>     That I have not the cloudy winds to keep
> Fresh for the opening of the morning's eye.
> Such dim-conceived glories of the brain
>     Bring round the heart an undescribable feud;
> So do these wonders a most dizzy pain,
>     That mingles Grecian grandeur with the rude
> Wasting of old Time—with a billowy main—
>     A sun—a shadow of a magnitude.

Keats's first sonnet reveals an awareness of neither the form of the Marbles nor their subject-matter. The poet's eye seems turned completely inward here. The grandeur of the Marbles recedes before the consciousness of his own poetic incapacities: the weakness of his own "spirit," the heavy weight of his own "mortality," the feud raging round his own "heart," his own "dizzy pain." Not the Marbles, but "my spirit" is of the essence here. The Marbles appear to have no reality external to that of the poet's subjective response. The art itself is seemingly more "undescribable" than the feud raging about his heart. What can apparently be portrayed, however, is the impression of the art, its psychological effect—how it weighs "on me"—how it reminds "me" of mortality, the "I" which must die. This self projected in the sonnet is wholly passive, so that the singer

himself appears almost as a receptacle into which external impressions are poured and with which he can do little. Not a hero, but a victim, he is a "sick Eagle" whose only luxury is "to weep," whose brain gives rise to glories which are only "dim-conceived."

The Marbles had been no less disarming for Haydon. Despite his painter's awareness of details and his need to discern the artistic principles at work, Haydon was also overwhelmed. He had observed the Marbles to study the groupings, the bones and muscles, an arm in repose, the horses' feet. He wants to deduce principles and learn from the Marbles; and yet, he emerges as a passive receptacle, no less than Keats. A "divine truth had blazed inwardly" upon the painter's mind. In a state of "perfect excitement," he was conscious of little else but the beat of his own heart. Even after a torturous evening and a nightmarish sleep, his enthusiasm had awakened him in a "fever of excitement." Seven years later, apparently, Haydon's excitement at the Marbles had not abated. His diary entries for November of 1815 repeat and develop his claim that the Marbles have become for him a link with divinity:

As I looked at the Lapitha who grapples a Centaur, I dwelt on it with more intensity than ever. Its beauty, its divinity, came over my soul like the influence of an angelic spirit, & totally abstracted from the World and its affairs, I caught myself actually uttering a prayer to it! I never was so acutely impressed before. I thank God my feelings are ripening & not getting cooler. Its influence came over me stronger & stronger & stronger till I could scarcely bear it. It felt as if a supernatural being was directing the beam of a burning lens to fire my soul. I hardly breathed. I imagined the red & fiery point was burning my heart, & then, as it were, suddenly sprung up in my feelings with an elasticity of Spirit, as if one had slipped out of one's skin. All night its Divinity has beamed to my brain—never was I so impressed with its inspiration.

Keats's second poem, *To B. R. Haydon, with the Foregoing Sonnet on the Elgin Marbles,* echoes the experience and the extravagant language of Haydon:

> For when men star'd at what was most divine
>  With browless idiotism—o'erwise phlegm—
> Thou hadst beheld the Hesperean shine
>  Of their star in the East, and gone to worship them.

Both Keats and Haydon respond to the Marbles with a subjectivism, a sentiment, and an ardor typical of the early nineteenth century. But this enthusiasm and intensity of feeling,
appropriate to the romantic tradition of aesthetics, seem in
grossest violation of the substance and intention of this zenith
of classical art. The modern reader, somewhat removed from
the aesthetics of romanticism, may scarcely note this disparity
without a vision of the Marbles and of the principles from
which they arose.

In 1816 the British government had bought from Lord Elgin,
Ambassador to Turkey, the greater portion of the 525-foot
frieze, fifteen metopes from the southern side, and the master-
pieces from the pediments of the Parthenon. Parts of the frieze
and the metopes from the other sides had been removed in the
fifth century when the building was dedicated to the Holy
Virgin; and after the Turkish conquest of 1456, only slight
remodeling proved necessary to transform the Christian church
into a mosque. The structure remained virtually intact until
1687, when Athens was besieged by Venetian artillery. An ex-
plosion of powder kegs stored in the mosque by the Turks left
the building and some of the southern metopes in ruins. A fifth
of the frieze is still missing, but more than half of the missing
segments can be reconstructed from sketches drawn in 1674
by an artist who accompanied the French Ambassador to
Constantinople.

Originally, three temples dedicated to Athena, patron goddess of war and wisdom, had stood on the sacred hill of Athens.
But after a sixty-year war against the Persians, Pericles was
impelled to revive the grandeur of Athens, the leading polis in
the Delian league. Work was entrusted to Phidias, a leading
craftsman, who superintended a crew of artists and builders in
the construction of new works of art. In 447–46 B.C., a new
temple to Athena began to rise high on the rocks dominating
the Attic plain. Some fifteen years later, work on the Parthenon
was complete. In his *Life of Pericles* Plutarch remarks that this
structure

was even then and at once antique; but in the freshness of its vigour it is,
even to the present day, recent and newly wrought. Such is the bloom of

perpetual newness, as it were, upon these works of his [Pericles], which makes them ever to look untouched by time, as though the unfaltering breath of an ageless spirit had been infused into them.

The sculpture and architecture of the Parthenon rendered with crystalline purity the artistic surge of the "golden age" in fifth-century B.C. Greece. With its poise, absolute restraint, and harmonious equilibrium, the beauty of this Pentelic marble structure immediately eclipsed that of all other buildings. Unlike the Gothic cathedrals of the Middle Ages, whose multiple arches conjoined in spiralling the worshipper heavenward into the infinite regions of God's mercies, the temple to Athena is at rest, sitting majestically atop the peak of man's world. Its horizontal planes curve slightly upward. Its vertical columns and walls curve inward. Extended in their curvature, all lines would meet in a pyramid, a little over a mile above. Thus, with almost perfect equilibrium, the duality of heaven and earth can be reconciled. An equipoise can be reached with the vertical and the horizontal, the divine and the mortal, the infinite and the finite. The tension between permanence and flux, being and becoming, dynamis and stasis is resolved.

This architectural repose is sustained in the frieze which was hewn around the building to represent the quadrennial procession of the Panathenaic Festival. Here, amidst a

ODE ON A
GRECIAN URN

> brede
> Of marble men and maidens overwrought

are lyrists and flute-players "for ever piping songs for ever new":

>             soft pipes, play on;
>   Not to the sensual ear, but, more endear'd,
>       Pipe to the spirit ditties of no tone . . .

Here are horsemen and charioteers,

>             that heifer lowing at the skies,
>   And all her silken flanks with garlands drest . . .

Here, surely, is the frieze that Keats was to project imaginatively upon an urn:

> Thou still unravish'd bride of quietness,
>    Thou foster-child of silence and slow time,
> Sylvan historian, who canst thus express
>    A flowery tale more sweetly than our rhyme:
> What leaf-fring'd legend haunts about thy shape
>    Of deities or mortals, or of both,
>       In Tempe or the dales of Arcady?
> What men or gods are these? What maidens loth?
>    What mad pursuit? What struggle to escape?
>       What pipes and timbrels? What wild ecstasy?

This momentary confusion at the opening of Keats's *Ode on a Grecian Urn*—between deities and mortals, the terrestrial grove of gods and the heaven-like dales for men—is somewhat understandable. On the frieze of the Parthenon, these two. groups are almost indistinguishable. Every mortal seems instilled with the holy aura of the ceremony, while the gods, descended from their celestial heights, await with Olympian calm the interpenetration of humans into their divine company.

Haydon was eventually to extract from the Marbles a set of principles. He was to see that what was apparent to the Greek might be hidden from the modern artist. We have "what the Greeks *had not,* an *antique* and a *system* to *mislead* us, and misplaced veneration and early habits to root out," he was to suggest. In both the *Examiner* and the *Champion* for March 1816 (then repeated verbatim in his thirteenth lecture, *On Painting and Design,* in 1844), Haydon was to enunciate with ardor and conviction his own rediscovery of the principles apparent in the Marbles: "the business of the artist is, to represent . . . so truly, as to excite in the mind of the spectator the exact association of the feelings intended to be conveyed." Although "the first great requisite, of course, is a capacity to feel a result," Haydon insisted that feeling alone never enabled the Greek sculptor to arrive at perfection. Feeling should also lead the way for understanding which must "ascertain the means of

producing in others what you feel yourself," but also the hand must acquire the technique of doing what you feel you want to do. Feeling is at once the instigator and the director.

Haydon was firmly convinced that this principle of feeling— what we have come to recognize as typically romantic and thus characteristic of the nineteenth century—was not just the mainstay of Greek art. It was fundamental to all great art.

Keats had no such delusions about Greek art—or about the possibilities of his own poetry. He was certainly not trying to imitate classical style in his sonnet, *On Seeing the Elgin Marbles,* any more than he was trying to affect Greek restraint in *Endymion.* As always, his concern is rather with sensations and unbridled passions, with a typical romantic breakthrough from restraint. Nowhere is this more clear than in his reformulation of the classical materials available for his own rendition of the Endymion myth. The vast lore on Endymion handed down by the ancients is restructured by Keats to accord with early nineteenth-century sensibilities, much as the Promethean myth is transformed by Shelley, and the Faustus theme by Goethe.

Despite their variants, the materials offered by the Greeks and Romans are fairly uniform in their presentation of the Endymion myth. According to Theocritus, Endymion is lulled to sleep by the moon; clearly wary of his powers of fertility, the goddess of chastity can preserve her own equanimity by kissing him only during his prolonged slumber. This is the version reputedly used by Sappho and by Nicander; but it is to be found in Cicero, who writes of the shepherd loved by the Lady Moon and sent by her into perpetual sleep; and in Ovid, who sings in *The Heroides* of the shepherd loved by Diana. Lucian tells the tale of Miua, a rival of Selene (the moon-goddess, later identified with Artemis and with Diana) who has also fallen in love with the shepherd. And to Endymion's surpassing beauty, Apollodorus attributes the fact that the moon goddess—ordinarily chaste and unmoved by men—has fallen in love with a mortal shepherd. Like the architecture and statuary of the Parthenon, the ancient myth offers an interfusion of the divine and the mortal. The eternal sleep thrust upon Endymion by his divine lover assures a relationship undisturbed by disquieting

passions, an equilibrium unshaken by the tremulous fevers of desire.

Keats was certainly aware of this standard version. During the weeks of September, 1817, when he himself was working in Oxford on that long narrative poem, he wrote for his young sister Fanny a child's account:

> Many Years ago there was a young handsome Shepherd who fed his flocks on a Mountain's Side called Latmus—he was a very contemplative sort of Person and lived solitry among the trees and Plains little thinking—that such a beautiful Creature as the Moon was growing mad in Love with him —However so it was; and when he was asleep on the Grass, she used to come down from heaven and admire him excessively from a long time; and at last could not refrain from carying him away in her arms to the top of that high Mountain Latmus while he was a dreaming—but I dare say [you] have read this and all the other beautiful Tales which have come down from the ancient times of that beautiful Greece.

*Ltr. to Fanny, 10 Sept. 1817*

Yet in Keats's poem the roles of mortal and deity are substantially altered. Not the moon-goddess, but the human shepherd is in ardent pursuit of love. Cynthia is no longer the symbol of chastity; through Keats, she emerges as the embodiment of eternality, immortality, perfect beauty—those ideals toward which all men would passionately aspire. The shepherd, ancient symbol of fertility, is transformed into an embodiment of impassioned ardor, ephemeral mortality, and passing beauty. In the hands of Keats, Endymion's intensive pursuit of immortal beauty becomes a reaffirmation of the mortal, earthly, sensuous world, where beauty can remain a joy forever. The shepherd seems to aim, not at poise, not at absolute restraint, not at harmonious equilibrium, but at

> Richer entanglements, enthralments far
> More self-destroying, leading, by degrees,
> To the chief intensity . . .

ENDYMION, *I*, *798–800*

Like his contemporaries, Keats assumed a liberty, a poetic license to alter the mythological facts as his imagination saw fit. Necessarily, the alteration was itself dependent upon a value

system which was basically nineteenth-century and romantic. He would be bound by none of the facts in his use of the Endymion myth; he would not subject himself to the tyranny of the eye in his sonnet, *On Seeing the Elgin Marbles*. It is equally unlikely that Keats would be constrained in his *Ode on a Grecian Urn* by a particular urn, or even by his vision of the Elgin Marbles themselves.

True, the Greek tragedians also worked with a common core of mythological materials and subjected them to multiple interpretations in accord with their own social, political, ethical, and artistic principles. But artistic liberties never implied a license to alter the given facts. In the whole of Greek literature, the question never arises whether Oedipus really killed his father or whether he will be thrust into exile for the patricide; whether Antigone really buried her brother and must die for it. These are ingredients already found within the mythological corpus. The main question confronting Sophocles and his audience rises from the dramatic structuring of these facts: how will they be arranged? what wisdom will they be made to reveal? how can they best be understood? And like the architecture and adornments of the Parthenon, *Oedipus Rex* and *Antigone* uphold the essence of *mesôtes,* that virtue which aims at a mean. After the extremes of passion and ignorance have been curbed, that equilibrium so essential to happiness can be restored.

Keats's nineteenth-century Endymion, who would move only to "the chief intensity" through rich entanglements and fierce enthrallments is certainly more romantic than Greek. He shares the principles and techniques of Haydon, and those of Girodet with his late eighteenth-century painting of a luxuriously indolent Endymion. He seems quite remote from ordering principles of Phidias with the Parthenon frieze, or of the unknown sculptor responsible for the second-century sarcophagus of Endymion, where the Periclean ideal has already hardened into a lifeless representation of detail. But then, Poussin's intellectualized painting of *Selene and Endymion,* staged like a Corneille drama, and André-Bardon's transformation of the ancient myth into a seductive game are equally remote from the earlier classical world.

Keats's shepherd is to be differentiated from the ideals of

Plato and Aristotle. And he is distinct from the values upheld in Sophocles' *Antigone* by Haemon, who urges his impassioned father to moderate the intensity of his emotions. Haemon recognizes that

> The wisest man will let himself be swayed
> By others' wisdom and relax in time.
> See how the trees beside a stream in flood
> Save, if they yield to force, each spray unharmed,
> But by resisting perish root and branch.
> The mariner who keeps his mainsheet taut,
> And will not slacken in the gale, is like
> To sail with thwarts reversed, keel uppermost.

Of course, Haemon is here voicing the principle of *mesôtes,* the self-control and self-restraint which is usually identified with Greek classicism. And yet, the situation to which he is reacting, the violent passion and excess of his father, is equally part of this classical world.

The Greeks were no strangers to passion and ardor. Creon, father of Haemon, storms before us in a fit of egocentric pride. Like Creon, and like all the other protagonists in Greek tragedy, Oedipus also gives vent to his emotional ardor, his petulance and excess. Unlike Keats and the romantics, however, Sophocles externalizes these feelings so that they are not simply indicative of inner turmoil. Through action, passions are placed in a well-illuminated foreground and made subservient to plot, the arrangements of incidents which were of primary importance to Aristotle. Thus, the character of Oedipus and of Creon is expressed, not only through their thoughts or words or feelings, but through their actions—that which can be most readily externalized and thrust into a foreground. What Oedipus does is for Sophocles of higher import than the conflicting feelings that rage within. Character is indeed man's fate, the daemon which determines his actions. But for the Greeks, character should not be determined by ardor or intensity of feeling. It should rather be determined by the ethical choices which control those warring feelings within, and upon which the character, and in turn the action, is itself dependent. Hence,

character must be subordinate to action; individual action must be subordinate to plot, the larger structuring; and diction, the externalization of thoughts and feelings, must be seen as subordinate to character. Aristotle's hierarchical division of the component parts of tragedy is indeed descriptive of the larger value system at work with the Greeks.

But Keats shares with the other romantics an unconcern with the externalization of action. Even his pieces written for the theatre—*Otho the Great* and *King Stephen*—neglect the primacy of action, just as the closet drama of Shelley and Byron, Coleridge and Lamb, fails in externalizing feelings. In *Endymion,* as in the sonnet *On Seeing the Elgin Marbles,* Keats's concern is with emotional response and psychological effect. Perhaps the closest the poet comes to the externalization of feeling is in the dramatizing of dialogue within the odes and some of the sonnets. But even here, where self confronts self, the speculative "conversation" lacks the dramatic situation so central to Shakespearean soliloquies or Browning's dramatic monologues. Haydon's principles, supposedly deduced from the Elgin Marbles themselves, could easily be seen as an articulation of the artistic principles at work with Keats, or with any of the other romantic poets. "The business of the artist," Haydon had written, "is, to represent . . . so truly, as to excite in the mind of the spectator the exact association of the feelings intended to be conveyed." The intensity with which Keats's Endymion feels his passions is paramount. Through the intensity of poetic language and the ardor of imaginative pursuit, the reader is invited to destroy his own identity, to project himself imaginatively and to merge with the protagonist of the poem. Similarly, the singer in *Ode to a Nightingale* is not content to remain in a world which is external to that of the bird; he would internalize that which is separate and distinct:

O for a beaker full of the warm South,
   Full of the true, the blushful Hippocrene,
      With beaded bubbles winking at the brim,
         And purple-stained mouth;
   That I might drink, and leave the world unseen,
      And with thee fade away into the forest dim:

> Fade far away, dissolve, and quite forget
> What thou among the leaves hast never known . . .

The mortal songster would be absorbed into the bird's world, just as the Elgin Marbles must themselves be absorbed into the subjective state embodied by the poet. Things, no less than actions, lose their value with Keats unless their external qualities can somehow be integrated within the self. In the beginning—but also in the end—there must be a relationship. As the poet himself was to explain the process, "every mental pursuit takes its reality and worth from the ardour of the pursuer— being in itself a nothing. . . ." The *it* must become absorbed into the *I* to form a greater, a holier *self*. Confronted with the estrangement of self and non-self, the certitudes of individual sensation and the baffling multeity of an alien world, the creative poet must either break down the separating barriers—or reconcile himself to solitude. *Ltr. to Bailey, 13 Mar. 1818*

With a theorist like Thomas Jefferson, that problem is enunciated with even greater clarity. "I consider our relations with others as constituting the boundaries of morality," Jefferson was to write in a letter to Thomas Law. "With ourselves we stand on the ground of identity, not of relation, which last, requiring two subjects, excludes self-love confined to a single one."

Even as the first book of *Endymion* was at the printer's, and months before the reviewers began their attack on this pseudo-classicism, Keats was himself writing to Haydon about the "many bits of the deep and sentimental cast" in the narrative poem. "The nature of *Hyperion* will lead me to treat it in a more naked and grecian Manner," he promises, "and the march of passion and endeavour will be undeviating." *Ltr. to Haydon, 23 Jan. 1818*

Yet, it was no more possible to reproduce the "grecian Manner" in Keats's day than it was to reproduce the Roman manner during the neo-Augustan age. Despite his emulation of the Marbles, Haydon himself could never produce an art that was not immediately recognizable as a romantic version of its classical prototype. Anne-Louis Girodet's execution of a new painting of Endymion, hailed by French critics during its first exhibition in 1792, seems to dissolve Grecian firmness of form with

a manner that is diffused and impressionistic. A movement in quite the other direction seems at work in *Selene and Endymion* by Michel François André-Bardon, who offers a late variation of the earlier neo-classic mode. Unlike Girodet whose figures are diffused with a sensuous abandonment, André-Bardon divests his figures of any real feeling. His Endymion is a man, pretending to be a shepherd; his Selene is a woman, affecting the pose of a goddess. Both figures are engaged in an amusing pastime—like Marie Antoinette, playing as shepherdess and dairy maid; like Pope's Belinda in *The Rape of the Lock,* with cosmetic powers which allow her to play the seductive game with artifice and wit.

The Wedgwood plaque of the same period, *Diana Visiting Endymion,* is no more in the "grecian Manner" than Keats's representation. Its frozen serenity is disrupted only by the agonies of an awakening shepherd with a Christ-like pose; but there is every indication that the goddess gliding effortlessly to his side will soon transform him into a shadowed silhouette as lifeless as she. Even Poussin's seventeenth-century version of the myth is distinct from the "grecian Manner," despite the arrangement of his characters in statuesque poses along lines parallel to the picture plane, in imitation of antique reliefs. His *Selene and Endymion* might well be the staging of a drama by Corneille, more consonant with the reasoned and intellectual French classicism of Boileau than the *mesôtes* of Aristotle or the interfusion of mortal and divine in Phidias.

Shelley picks up the Promethean myth, only to convert it into a Godwinian form. Etruria, the new pottery factory opened in 1769 by Josiah Wedgwood, succeeded in transfusing (as Coleridge was to recognize) for daily domestic use in an egalitarian society the fairest forms, but never the dynamic spirit, of ancient Greece. Even in a work as mature as the *Ode on a Grecian Urn,* where sentiment has indeed given way to a "more naked and grecian Manner," the aesthetics are still nineteenth-century and romantic.

Of course Keats's artistic principles were more immediately derived from assumptions he shared with his contemporaries: Haydon, in painting; Hazlitt and Leigh Hunt, in criticism; Wordsworth and Shelley, in poetry. His values may appear

somewhat remote from those enunciated by Plato and Aristotle, implicit in the tragedies of Sophocles, and apparent in the structure of the Parthenon.

Still, these aesthetic principles of the early nineteenth century were deeply rooted in ancient Greece. They had their origins in Greek art, in Greek myth, and in Greek philosophy. For Keats and for Shelley, for Byron, Hazlitt, and Haydon, the turn to classical materials and the emulation of classical form was more than a passing fad. Like the uncouth swain in Milton's *Lycidas,* the romantics were impelled to move toward fresh woods and pastures new. Keats could not avoid taking with him, in whatever form, a more ancient culture as it had infiltrated the Western world over a period of two thousand years or more.

# 2
# Craft vs. Inspiration:
# The Socratic Plea

The artistic principles of Plato—so kindly, so regretfully, but so unalterably opposed to that impassioned muse that divorces itself from reason—are perhaps nowhere as lucidly expounded as in the *Ion*. Toward the middle of this most graceful dialogue, the visitor from Epidaurus, having already spoken at length about the gifts of Homer, begins to wonder why it is that he can talk better and have more to say about Homer than about other poets. In reply to his visitor's encomium about the greatness of this ancient writer, Socrates starts to draw the now familiar distinction between those gifts of speaking or singing or writing which are arts and those which arise when the individual is inspired or possessed:

. . . This is not an art in you, whereby you speak well on Homer, but a divine power. . . . In the same manner also the Muse inspires men herself, and then by means of these inspired persons the inspiration spreads to others, and holds them in a connected chain. For all the good epic poets utter all those fine poems not from art, but as inspired and possessed, and the good lyric poets likewise; just as the Corybantian worshippers do not dance when in their senses, so the lyric poets do not indite those fine songs in their senses, but when they have started on the melody and rhythm they begin to be frantic, and it is under possession. . . . For a poet is a light and winged and sacred thing, and is unable ever to indite until he has been

inspired and put out of his senses, and his mind is no longer in him: every man, whilst he retains possession of that, is powerless to indite a verse or chant an oracle. Seeing then that it is not by art that they compose and utter so many fine things about the deeds of men . . . but by a divine dispensation, each is able only to compose that to which the Muse has stirred him. . . . For not by art do they utter these things, but by divine influence; since, if they had fully learnt by art to speak on one kind of theme, they would know how to speak on all. And for this reason God takes away the mind of these men and uses them as his ministers, just as he does soothsayers and godly seers, in order that we who hear them may know that it is not they who utter these words of great price, when they are out of their wits, but that it is God himself who speaks and addresses us through them.

Although Socrates speaks very little in this particular passage or elsewhere about the art of poetry, it is relatively clear that art—or *technê*, the Greek term he uses repeatedly here—must be based upon human, rational principles. The poet (a *poiêtês* or maker) is a particular kind of craftsman. As an artisan, a *technitês*, he has a learned skill, a craft based upon principles, a knowledge of techniques. Increasingly, since the late eighteenth century, the term *art* has had non-functional and highly eclectic connotations which set it apart from the mechanics of practical and pragmatic technology, just as philosophic knowledge has been distinguished increasingly from scientific. But this dualism is decidedly absent from the Greeks in general and from Plato in particular. *Technê* or *craft* was equally applicable to the training of a boy, the moulding of a vase, the building of a temple, the construction of a poem. The distinction Socrates raises here is not between a non-functional *art* and a functional *technology*. Rather, he is distinguishing knowledge from inspiration, human from divine, the rational from the irrational, as the bases of art. Insofar as man is a rational animal, all *technê* —the craft by which his reason is revealed—is indicative of knowledge and therefore the essence of human virtues.

The inspired poet, moved by a divinity within him, is in the language of Socrates *entheos:* the gods are within him. His own reason and will having been subordinated to those of the divinities moving within and directing, he is inspired (the *spiritus* moves within) and enthused (by *theistic* forces). Like Corybantian revellers and Dionysian maidens, he is not in posses-

sion of his mind—that is, he is not operating as humans should ideally function. If he is "possessed," then he is "put out of his senses, and his mind is no longer in him." Thus, art or the product of man's mind is to be distinguished from those works which are evoked by "divine influence" and "divine power."

For the reader familiar with the Socratic dialogues, this particular passage in the *Ion* must be interpreted, not as a eulogy of inspired poetry, but rather as a lament that by the interference of the gods who use us as their ministers and diviners, their prophets and interpreters, we are prevented from fulfilling our human capacity. Like Plato's other dialogues, the *Ion* upholds the importance of the intellectual, the volitional, the reasoned and "examined life" which is alone worth living. As a consequence, Homer, together with other writers of epic and lyric verse, is regrettably banned from the republic, where philosopher-kings must rule according to their clearest and most reasoned apprehension of the One: the True, the Good, the Beautiful. Homer is acknowledged to be the greatest of poets and first among the writers of tragedy. Yet, only hymns to the gods and measured praises of virtuous men are to be allowed in the ideal state, for the honeyed muse can plant within man's soul an evil constitution. She can indulge the irrational which has small discernment of good and evil, the greater and the less. Once she enters the republic, "pleasure and pain will be lords of your city, instead of law and that which shall from time to time have approved itself to the general reason as the best." The greatest poets, for all their madness, may be in closest touch with the One, but by ignoring their function as men—as rational, volitional beings—they would uphold madness as a model for those who would learn how to live. And after all, the humanistic problem, the problem of how to live and how to die, is what is paramount in Plato. The function of man, bounded by his corporeal frame which would drag him earthward against the larger strivings of his soul, is to reconcile the contradictory and paradoxical claims of the white steed and the dark, pure mind and misguided senses.

The romantics of the early nineteenth century were concerned no less with the humanistic problem, the problem of how to live and how to die. But with their apprehensions about

mind, which during the preceding era had become increasingly identified with the cold precision of mechanical and mathematical reason, the romantics cast about for a more reliable source for knowledge. Correspondingly, they sought a new determinant for art based, not upon *a priori* principles, but upon an immediacy of expression, an intensity of feeling about which Socrates had been so apprehensive. As a result, art came no longer to be identified with *technê*. It was rather identified with *aesthêsis*—what the Greeks would have associated with perception and sensation. And the new antithesis of art was no longer *entheos*, but *nous*—mind with its cognitive faculties, its powers of analysis and conceptualizing. In this curiously inverted set of values, the language of art, Socrates notwithstanding, was indeed to become the language of enthusiasm. Not law and reason, but pleasure and pain seemed to be upheld as rulers of the new state.

Keats's concern with pleasure—like Wordsworth's and Shelley's—is not limited to sensation alone; it gravitates about his concern with reality, with beauty, and with knowledge. Although this concern may not correspond with Socrates', Keats is intent upon the same humanistic values. He offers a variant of Socratic classicism, just as both Aristotle and Horace offer their variants. Thus, in the tenth book of the *Nichomachean Ethics*, Aristotle distinguishes between base pleasures and proper pleasures in the development of man's potential, his activities which aim at happiness. With Horace, as well, pleasure is an essential ingredient. In *Ars Poetica*, Horace had written of the joint aim of the poet, *aut prodesse aut delectare*, to combine teaching with pleasure, the useful with the delightful. Horatian *delectare* is of course distinct from Keatsian pleasure, dependent as it is upon the seeming or proper, what is fitting, useful, and appropriate. For Horace, the true source of delight is found within the proper, and the prime essential for the appropriate is wisdom: the ability to know what is fitting.

Horatian knowledge is not consonant with Socratic knowledge—but then neither is it to be identified with the kind of knowledge Keats invokes for *Hyperion*, when he urges that a distinction be made between "the false beauty proceeding from art, and . . . the true voice of feeling." The appeal he makes

*Ltr. to Reynolds, 21 Sept. 1819*

for *Lamia* seems to be based upon sensory stimuli alone: "I am
*Ltr. to George &*
*Georgiana,*
*18 Sept. 1819* certain there is that sort of fire in it which must take hold of
people in some way—give them either pleasant or unpleasant
sensation. What they want is a sensation of some sort." Actually, Keats would conjure up the same sensorial powers that
Wordsworth had appealed to in his preface to the second edition of *Lyrical Ballads,* where he had argued that "our
thoughts . . . are indeed the representatives of all our past
feelings," therefore good poetry "is the spontaneous overflow of
powerful feelings." But feeling alone is no more desirable for
Wordsworth than for Keats. "Powerful feelings" can be produced only "by a man who, being possessed of more than usual
organic sensibility, had also thought long and deeply," Wordsworth insists. And Keats's statement about "pleasant or unpleasant sensation" in *Lamia* must be countered by his letter to
*Ltr. to Reynolds,*
*11 July 1819* Reynolds which expresses "great hopes of success, because I
make use of my Judgment more deliberately than I yet have
done. . . ."

With much the same view of pleasurable sensations as the
source of truth and knowledge, William Hazlitt had argued in
his essay *On Reason and Imagination* that

> with respect to moral truth (as distinct from mathematical), whether a
> thing is good or evil, depends on the quantity of Passion, of feeling, of
> pleasure and pain connected with it. . . . Passion, in short, is the essence,
> the chief ingredient in moral truth; and the warmth of passion is sure to
> kindle the light of imagination on the objects around it.

Coleridge had tried to make the same distinction between
knowledge arrived at through reason and that achieved
through the emotions, when in his preliminary essay *On the
Principles of Genial Criticism* he had contra-distinguished poetry from science. "The common essence of all arts consists in
the excitement of emotion for the immediate purpose of pleasure through the medium of beauty." Although the sciences
may give pleasure, and the arts may lead to important truths,
the immediate aim and primary purpose of science is truth and
possible utility, Coleridge was to insist. Several decades before,
Edmund Burke had developed a whole aesthetic of sublimity
about ideas of pain and terror, the strongest emotion which the

mind is capable of feeling. For Burke, the passions are sympathetic and social, as well as selfish and self-preserving. Pleasure and pain affect the heart, but they also are applicable to qualities of the mind. Powerful, intense, overwhelming, the passions alone are for Burke capable of transporting us into the sublime flights that can be achieved through sensation, through pleasure.

The age of Pericles was not unconcerned with these sensations and pleasures. In a play like *The Bacchae,* Pentheus and his followers are led to ruin and destruction as a consequence of their blasphemous attempts to outlaw the orgiastic rites of Dionysius and to keep the state pure and holy. Although the denial of the sensual and the irrational, the suppression of frenzied madness and divine enthusiasm, emerge as the tragic flaw for this Euripidean hero, it is reasonably clear that Euripides is not upholding divine madness as an ideal. He is here condemning as madness that view of man which blinds itself to the irrational in his nature and would uphold only the purity of the mind. If true moderation is to be achieved, Euripidean wisdom demands an alliance of these two sides of our nature: body and soul, passions and intellect—what Socrates earlier had described as our dark and white steeds; and what Nietzsche was later to perceive as the Dionysian and the Apollonian.

Apparent in *Oedipus*—if the judgment of Aristotle is sustained—is the wisdom of a master craftsman like Sophocles who can reveal a thorough knowledge of the tragedian's *technê* when, almost like a demi-god, he can rouse in his spectators the lowest passions, pity and fear; and then, having roused these feelings, he can equally effect their proper purgation. With much the same design, Aristotle aims in his *Rhetoric* and his *Poetics* at the orator and the playwright, those *technités* who must learn to arouse the passions to serve the ultimate good, that happiness toward which all men aim. As with Socrates, the subordination of passions to a given ethical end is mandatory. The dramatist—like the rhetorician, the poet, the politician—should be concerned with the teaching of values. Sophoclean truth is not dependent, as with Hazlitt, upon the intensity of passion; passions for the Greek tragedian are rather subordinated to the ends of truth, and feelings are harnessed in the

service of good and evil. Drawn into an identification of self
with Oedipus, the spectator himself learns how to live, how to
find happiness, how better to rise to the divine heights of which
man is capable. Purged of his improper emotions, his pity for
Oedipus and his fear for himself, the spectator achieves a
higher knowledge; he learns to realize his greatest potentialities
as man. He has better learned to make his own choices upon
which his actions ought to depend. Thus, the golden mean
becomes accessible even to the most brazen slave. And by examining in Aristotle's *Poetics* the errors of other *technitês*, the
would-be tragedian can learn how to fulfill himself, how best to
realize the potency of his art: what is possible according to the
laws of dramatic probability or necessity.

Even Socrates, with his distrust of the senses and his insistence
that the greatest good can be derived from the mind, recognizes
that pure thought is an ideal toward which mortals must strive,
even though they may rarely achieve it with their corporeal
frame. Rather than cutting the traces of the dark steed who
would plunge him into error and ignorance, and following only
the lofty surges of the soul, the wise charioteer must learn to
reconcile the dark steed with the white. His strength of will
keeps his passions in rein, just as in Plato's republic the workers
must learn to subordinate their individual wills and their bodily passions to the larger functioning of the state. As long as the
worker or the soldier follows the dictates of the philosopher-
kings whose apprehension of the One is most lucid, the soul of
the state and the soul of man are united in their striving toward
the ideal. Socrates' concern is always epistemological. He seeks
an understanding, a knowledge derived from the world of pure
form, of how man can best achieve in this world, by his own
powers and with his own faculties, a fulfillment of his human
capacities. The best art must arise from and be coincident with
the fullest knowledge. Beauty in the world of sensations is that
which imitates most closely beauty in the world of pure form.

Thus, the Socratic emphasis upon *technê* was primarily—but
not wholly—intellectual; it was concerned with human knowledge and its capacity to achieve divine heights—with what the
newer classicism of the early nineteenth century was equally
concerned. In many ways, that later movement comes closer to

the ideals of Periclean Athens than the mechanical and mathematical variant offered during the "neo-classical" period of the late seventeenth and early eighteenth centuries, when a somewhat different alignment of reason and sensation, mind and feeling, had ordered the attitudes and values which determined the visible form of life and art.

The visible forms of Plato and Sophocles are, of course, distinct from those projected by Keats and Wordsworth. For the nineteenth-century romantic, knowledge was perceptual, rather than conceptual; it was achieved through the senses, rather than through mind alone. Nevertheless, it was concerned with knowledge as a means of ordering the visible forms of reality. Romantic knowledge follows *a posteriori* upon experience and is achieved through experience. It does not, as with Socrates, precede the operations of a conceptualizing mind which can only come upon or discover what already has an *a priori* existence. It insists that the knowledge of immediate pleasure cannot be disassociated from the knowledge of far-reaching truths. Typically, true craftsmanship does not demand of Wordsworth that the poet begin with certain truths, of which the poem itself is once or twice removed. The Wordsworthian poet begins with the particulars of an isolated experience that offers an immediate pleasure and therefore the assurance of knowledge. Indeed, all experience leads the poet to the same truths about the "Wisdom and Spirit of the universe," which provide for individual images and individual forms an "everlasting motion,"

> a sense sublime
> Of something far more deeply interfused,
> Whose dwelling is the light of setting suns,
> And the round ocean and the living air,
> And the blue sky, and in the mind of man;
> A motion and a spirit, that impels
> All thinking things, all objects of all thought,
> And rolls through all things.

Poetic craft in Keats is no less arbitrary. Like Wordsworth, Keats must necessarily begin with a particular urn or cricket,

legend or vision. Although the particulars lead him to the same knowledge, he would not begin with that knowledge. It must, rather, emerge from his wrestling with the particulars, from his experience with the urn or cricket. Keatsian knowledge does not reside within the thing, to be discovered as a separate reality. It emerges from the individual's *techné*, from his intensity of experience with the thing.

Socrates' ideas about craft were scarcely a new notion appearing for the first time in fifth-century B.C. Athens. In recording the words of his teacher, Plato was simply developing his own craft, putting into a system ideas which permeate the Homeric epics and the vast body of mythological lore of ancient Greece. In that lore, gods and goddesses move with ease in the mortal world, just as men and women interpenetrate with almost equal facility the divine regions. Interrelationships are physical and sexual, as well as social and psychological. Wise or courageous, crafty or strong, the Greek hero is accorded no higher compliment than the suspicion that the divine gods have had a skilled hand in his making. The flaming torch stolen from the heavens by Prometheus against the edict of Zeus is upheld by Aeschylus as the greatest resource of mortals—the fount of knowledge, the teacher of crafts. That which was the property of the gods can indeed pass into the hands of men. Within limitations, the reaching for divine knowledge is for the Greek the highest virtue, for through those heavenly arts and skills, mortals can indeed become like unto the gods themselves.

Although the ancient Greek seemed to delight in being human, he very much recognized that his humanity was enhanced by interaction with the divine. Prometheus is portrayed by Aeschylus not at all unsympathetically for his aid to the new divinities, those "upstart gods" whom he has "endowed with reason," and for whom he has devised every art and science:

First of all, though they had eyes to see, they saw to no avail; they had ears, but understood not; but, like to shapes in dreams, throughout their length of days, without purpose they wrought all things in confusion. Knowledge had they neither of houses built of bricks and turned to face the sun, nor yet of work in wood; but dwelt beneath the ground like swarming ants, in sunless caves. They had no sign either of winter or of flowery spring or of fruitful summer, whereon they could depend, but in everything they

wrought without judgment, until such time as I taught them to discern the risings of the stars and their settings, ere this ill distinguishable. Aye, and numbers, too, chiefest of sciences, I invented for them, and the combining of letters, creative mother of the Muses' arts, wherewith to hold all things in memory. I, too, first brought brute beasts beneath the yoke to be subject to the collar and the pack-saddle, that they might bear in men's stead their heaviest burdens; and to the chariot I harnessed horses and made them obedient to the rein, to be an adornment of wealth and luxury. 'Twas I and no one else that contrived the mariner's flaxen-winged car to roam the sea.

Despite the good that he has brought into being, Prometheus himself is not without *hamartia,* the excessive pride and treacherously impassioned ardor which threatens with dangerous confusion to violate the core of his own immortal being. But he is cautioned repeatedly throughout the drama to purge his excesses, just as Aeschylus himself orders the materials of the myth to provoke his audience into an excessive emotional state which can eventually be purged.

To view the Greeks as the epitome of reason and order is a distortion, as we have come increasingly to recognize; for the divine madness which Plato was disparaging was rooted in Greek religion, imbedded in all their drama, made visible even on their pottery and shields and paintings where Dionysius and his companions are frequently depicted in all their orgiastic frenzy. It was at work in the *Ion,* when the visitor from Epidaurus revealed his unabashed enthusiasm for Homer; it was at work in the Athenian court of five hundred and one jurors who were immune to the plea for reason and dispassionate objectivity, as recorded in Plato's *Apology,* and who voted the death penalty for Socrates. Indeed, their recognition of the passions was to become the core of their humanism, for the ancient Greeks were concerned, not just with the expression of the passions, but with a quantitative analysis of when passion is necessary and desirable, and when it is dangerous and treacherous. Unfortunately, we tend still to derive our notions about classicism more from Pope and from Corneille than from Sophocles; less from Periclean Athens and more from the neo-classical period of the late seventeenth and early eighteenth centuries.

Like all great movements, the Periclean age was short-lived. By the second half of the fourth century, the proportions were

visibly altering. An emotional subjectivism and a new emphasis on pathos introduced an attitude which was eventually to culminate in the frieze of Pergamon, the Laocoon, the *Peri Hupsous* of Longinus. This was a subjectivism which the late eighteenth century was to seize upon as the basis for a new aesthetics —and to misunderstand as the height of ancient Greek culture. This late Hellenic movement was classicism still, though Plato would have disavowed its principles, no less than he would have disavowed the "classical" principles of Pope and Corneille.

In the Socratic dialogue, no less than in *Oedipus* or the frieze of the Parthenon, is a partial fulfillment of an art form that was political, ethical, metaphysical at its core. But for Socrates, as for his contemporaries in fifth-century B.C. Athens, this was an art in which *technê* was to be distinguished from what the nineteenth century was later to identify with *aesthêsis*—what Socrates would probably have disparaged as divine madness.

# 3
# Classicism in Renaissance Poetics

Built on the foundations of Athenian civilization, the new romantic order seems more immediately indebted for its structure and its ideal to the politics of Rousseau and Jefferson, and less to *The Republic* of Plato; more to the "sublime" of Edmund Burke and the "picturesque" of William Gilpin, than to Phidias, Sophocles, or even Longinus. Yet, the classicism emerging from Keats and his contemporaries—in harmony with a new egalitarianism, a new brotherhood of man, a new social and political order—was really not too far removed from the "examined life" of Plato or the *mesôtes* of Aristotle. In many ways the early nineteenth-century romantics represent a mutation of classicism. Like Renaissance humanists, they engaged in a protestant movement. They were protesting against the way in which the values of ancient Greece and Rome were being neglected and distorted—much as the Renaissance humanists had extended their protest against the misuse of classical standards under the aegis of the medieval church.

Of course, classicism had never really been neglected during the Middle Ages. Classical motifs had been invested with Christian values; classical themes were expressed by religious figures in a theological setting. Plato could be subsumed by Augustine,

Aristotle by Aquinas. In medieval iconography, Plato, Seneca, and Aristotle might emerge as the Blessed Trinity. Orpheus could be fused with a representation of David. The rape of Europa could be interpreted pictorially as the prefigurement of salvation through Christ. Aphrodite, mother of *erós* and symbol of fleshly beauty, could be portrayed as a courtly lady strumming upon her lute, transformed into the embodiment of *agapé*, the purity of God's love for man. The moon's love for Endymion might suggest a *coniunctio* of soul and body, mind and heart, so that the amorous rays of the moon, coming to caress the sleep of mortals, might be analogized to the love of Christ who sheds his blessing upon the weak and sinful.

In the Second Tractate of the *Convivio*, Dante had set down four ways by which writings ought properly to be expounded with learning and with knowledge so that truth might emerge beyond "the strict limits of the letter." For Dante knowledge was a ready compound of classical and Christian:

. . . It should be known that writings can be understood and ought to be expounded chiefly in four senses. The first is called literal, and this is that sense that does not go beyond the strict limits of the letter; the second is called allegorical, and this is disguised under the cloak of such stories, and is a truth hidden under a beautiful fiction. Thus, Ovid says that Orpheus with his lyre made beasts tame, and trees and stones move toward himself; that is to say that the wise man by the instrument of his voice makes cruel hearts grow mild and humble, and those who have not the life of Science and of Art move to his will, while they who have no rational life are as it were stones. . . .

The third sense is called moral; and this sense is that which teachers ought as they go through writings intently to watch for their own profit and that of their hearers; as in the Gospel when Christ ascended the Mount to be transfigured, we may be watchful of His taking with Himself the three apostles out of the twelve; whereby morally it may be understood that for the most secret affairs we ought to have few companions.

The fourth issue is called anagogic, that is, above the senses; and this occurs when a writing is spiritually expounded which even in the literal sense by the things signified likewise gives intimation of higher matters belonging to the eternal glory; as can be seen in that song of the prophet which says that, when the people of Israel went up out of Egypt, Judea was made holy and free. And although it is plain that this is true according to the letter, that which is spiritually understood is no less true, namely, that when the soul issues forth from sin she is made holy and free as mistress of herself.

Later, in his tenth *epistola* to Can Grande della Scala, Dante described more fully this freedom of the soul through issuance from sin as "the departure of the holy soul from the slavery of this corruption to the liberty of eternal glory." Apparently, the art of the *Commedia*—one foot in the Middle Ages, another in the Renaissance—was dictated by the same assumptions, for in this epistle to his young patron, the aging poet lay bare his intentions with this major work, where "the end of the whole and the part is to remove those living in this life from the state of misery and lead them to the state of felicity."

Keats too was to look upon his art as a means of achieving "the state of felicity." But the homocentric orientation of the nineteenth-century poet sought out a happiness "independant *Ltr. to Bailey,* of the great Consolations of Religion." Repelled by the com- *3 Nov. 1817* mon notion of Christian salvation, Keats would find felicity through man's interaction with the *things* of beauty which are a joy forever: the happiness of some light-winged songster in the trees; the happy love embossed upon a Grecian urn that offers all one needs to know on earth; the song of grasshoppers and crickets, that poetry of earth which never ceases. Derived through the world of sensation, Keatsian happiness emerges from "the Beautiful—the poetical in all things." From the beginning, it must be dependent upon man's devices, not God's.

Thus, when Keats re-interprets and re-writes the Endymion myth, he depends upon his personal strivings to charge the traditional materials with a new and more meaningful signifi-cance. In the hands of the romantic poet, a permutation of classicism emerges. We tend now to speak of "romanticisms," rather than "romanticism," cognizant of the multiple varieties at work. With equal propriety, we ought to speak of "classi-cisms," rather than "classicism." In their day, Boileau and Dryden managed to invoke a form of classicism distinct from that which Keats was later to develop, but equally distinguisha-ble from that of Sophocles and Aristotle or, indeed, from the form apparent in Dante or Shakespeare. Through the prism of late seventeenth-century optics, Boileau and Dryden man-aged to subordinate the dynamics of the Periclean *media via* to their own vision of the Supreme Architect as mechanical, ra-tional, orderly, geometric—and produced a variant that has

been called "neo-classicism." Different in kind, this is no less a classical variant than that produced in the late sixteenth century by John Lyly, who was working with a form resembling the Christian humanism of Machiavelli and Pico, Michelangelo and Pomponazzi and Shakespeare.

Employing the historical facts at his disposal, the Endymion myth Keats found recorded in Sandys' Ovid, in Tooke or Lemprière, Lyly managed to reformulate the materials in accord with his late sixteenth-century value system. The result is a Renaissance variant of Greek classicism. The proportions have altered visibly; nevertheless, they are still recognizable as classical. Lyly's *Endymion, or The Man in the Moon* is as subject as Dante's *Commedia* to polysemous interpretation, although Lyly's Renaissance allegory is not subjected to the theocentric orientation of the medieval church.

On the literal level, a spell of endless sleep is cast over Lyly's Endymion—but through the machinations of Tellus, goddess of the earth, who is jealous of his affection for the moon-goddess Cynthia. After twenty years of sleep, Endymion is awakened and rejuvenated through the combined efforts of his friend Eumenides and his love Cynthia.

On the allegorical level, as has been so frequently suggested, Lyly is possibly portraying the rivalry of Elizabeth (Cynthia) and Mary, Queen of Scots (Tellus) ; or the aspirations of James VI of Scotland (Endymion) to the English throne; or the relations of Sir Philip Sidney (Eumenides) with his uncle Leicester and his love Penelope Rich (Semele).

On the moral level, the arrangement of incidents is concentrated in true Elizabethan fashion upon the dilemma faced by Eumenides when, in search of the sleeping Endymion, he is granted a single wish from the magical fountain. To ask for his love Semele is a betrayal of his friendship for Endymion; and to inquire after his friend Endymion is a betrayal of his love for Semele. Wisely, he follows the counsel of an old sage who contrasts ephemeral lust for woman and eternal love for man. Actually, this same contrast between lust and love, temporal and eternal, mortal and divine, bestial and heavenly, had been developed since the opening of the play. Endymion's own love of Cynthia was a love of eternal virtue embodied in the chaste

moon-goddess. A minor character, Corsites, is torn between lust and virtue, like Eumenides, but Corsites obviously makes the wrong choice and must be punished. Eumenides is eventually rewarded with Semele because he knows that mortal passing love is inferior to divine eternal virtue. And even Cynthia, whose chaste lips have never been touched, agrees to sacrifice herself to another and to reveal true virtue, when she bestows upon Endymion the kiss that will awaken him from his slumbers.

Lyly's reassessment of the myth offers no physical merging of mortal and divine, except for the single kiss. For the Greek, this physical interaction is made possible only to those few with beauty of body and soul—Anchises, Ganymede, Psyche, Endymion. For the medieval Christian, the company of the divine is also held forth as a possibility, though only for the pure of body and soul. Lyly is not arranging his classical materials to reveal Divine Love infused within mortal man, so essential to the medieval lives of saints. Like a typical Renaissance man, Eumenides is confronted with a choice of rising to divine spheres or degenerating into a bestial form. Wisely, he sees the chaste love of friendship as a higher form than lust for woman. With an ending that offered a travesty to medieval canons, Lyly rewards him ultimately with the love of Semele, for Eumenides has revealed that he knows the proper place for lust. Neither angel nor devil, Eumenides can apparently order his middle world so that terrestrial and heavenly are in proper proportion to one another, in correspondence with the ordered world of nature, where the various stars and planets all pursue their ordered course. Endymion, in his singular pursuit of the immortal Cynthia, has already made his choice; but because he ignores his own mortality, he necessarily opens the way to suffering. At the opposite extreme, Corsites pursues only lust, stifling the celestial strain imbedded within him, as in all men; and he too must suffer.

Actually, the balanced proportion which Eumenides achieves in Lyly's play, the correspondence with the ordered world of nature, is at the core of Gian Battista Cima's painting of *Endymion and the Moon*. Here, in typical Renaissance manner, man's world and the world of nature are balanced in harmony:

the lines of the low diaphanous moon echo in reverse the curve of the recumbent fleshy body; the curls of Endymion's hair and the fringes and scallops of his garments echo the decorative flora and fauna; the shepherd's sleep is echoed by the dormant animal world. Rubens is trying to effect this order—a system of correspondences which we have come to identify with the Renaissance—in his portrayal of the same myth. Although Rubens uses a pose somewhat reminiscent of Michelangelo's *Creation of Adam,* the power and vitality so crucial to divinity in the Sistine Chapel painting are here weak and ineffective. Thus, the contrast between active divinity and passive mortality simply do not work in Rubens. Like Cima's pudgy Italianate youth, Rubens' figures are fleshy and sensuous; only the horses are vibrant and quivering with life. Indeed, a diagonal line drawn from the upper left would move us from the greatest activity to the least, from the divine world to the mundane, centering on the awakening touch of Diana's hand. Rubens' problem may be that he relies too much upon color to effect his system of correspondences, for the golden glow of Diana's chariot, her gown and hair, permeates the natural world of trees and bushes and ground. Even Endymion's body begins to assume the golden tinges of divinity, while the spiritual pallor of Diana's skin and her horses is contrasted with the blood-red gown which hangs about the shepherd's mortal frame. This harmonious balance which Cima achieves and which Rubens aims at—what Lyly's *Endymion* is working with, also—is quite distinct from the infusion of divine within the mortal and of the human within the celestial, revealed in the Elgin Marbles. And of course it is quite distinct from the ordering at work in Keats's handling of the myth.

Eumenides and Endymion both achieve some degree of happiness in Lyly's play, because of their human capacities and despite their human limitations. They have managed to achieve the divine heights of which man alone, by his very nature, is capable. Like Machiavelli's prince, they have shed lustre upon themselves, though no less upon their Creator and upon all mankind.

Keats's nineteenth-century Endymion achieves no such ideal. The ends have perceptibly altered. Classicism has assumed an-

other form. In an early speech to Peona about the nature of felicity, Endymion inquires:

> Wherein lies happiness? In that which becks
> Our ready minds to fellowship divine,
> A fellowship with essence; till we shine,
> Full alchemiz'd, and free of space.

ENDYMION, *I*,
*777–780*

But happiness for Keats's Endymion consists not in the knowing reconciliation of love and lust, the learned techniques of ordering divine and bestial, that deliberate circumscribing of thoughts and passions which for Montaigne is more essential for greatness of soul than pressing forward and upward. For Keats's Endymion, happiness seems to consist of rich entanglements and ardent pursuits, enthrallments self-destroying, what Keats himself was to describe as that "intensity, capable of making all disagreeables evaporate." Like Ludolph in the final scene of *Otho the Great*, Endymion is aware that

*Ltr. to George &
Tom,
21 Dec. 1817*

> pendent lamps and chandeliers are bright
> As earthly fires from dull dross can be cleansed;
> Yet could my eyes drink up intenser beams
> Undazzled . . .

What distinguishes Keats's Endymion from Lyly's is a modified relationship between feeling and knowledge, imagination and learning, sensation and *techné*.

Still, despite his differences from Lyly and from the formulators of Renaissance art, Keats shares with this earlier group a system of classical values aimed at reviving the essential homocentricity of the Greeks, stressing not the greater grandeur of God, but the divine capacities of man. With the early nineteenth-century romantic and with the humanists emerging from the *quattrocento*, artistic values derive from man's potential as a second deity, a mortal creator aspiring to divine heights.

For the Renaissance, God as First Cause may set all things into motion; yet man with his learning may in this world of nature effect a correspondence to the eternal harmonies dis-

cernible in His world. Although God may be omnipotent in His realm, man has the capacity within the world of nature to seek godhead—or to fall from it. "All things have conspired to your greatness; the rest you must now do yourselves," Machiavelli advises his prince. "God does not want to do everything for us, so as not to deprive us of free will nor take from us that portion of glory which is ours." While we can rarely control the vagaries of fortune, we can develop our own learning and wisdom, and to some extent we can control our own fate by imitating the examples of great men in history: this is the advice of the author of *The Prince*. With a similar perspective, Pico della Mirandola stresses in his famed *Oration on the Dignity of Man* that men are unlike all other beings in nature who are constrained and limited within the bounds of Divine Law. But through knowledge and will, men can ordain for themselves. Neither earthly nor celestial, neither mortal nor immortal, man alone possesses the power to degenerate into the lower, brutish forms of life, or to be reborn into the higher and divine realm. Pomponazzi is similarly cognizant of the mean that man occupies between the terrestrial and the heavenly. Therefore, in his treatise *On the Immortality of the Soul,* he urges that man use the power he has to assume whatever nature he wishes, for he has within him both beast and man, the sensate and the insensate. Like Mark Antony, man's legs can bestride the ocean, his reared arm crest the world; but at the same time, his dotage can transform him into Cleopatra's fool. Like Macbeth, once noble and brave, man can degenerate into the dead butcher.

These are assumptions inherent in Scaliger's *Poetics,* where by virtue of his creative act, the artist reveals the potential of transforming himself almost into "a second deity." Scaliger's Renaissance artist does not bend his own will to conform with the Divine, like Dante's; nor does he function like Aristotle's *technitês,* as midwife to the world of matter, bringing into being the potentiality of form, assisting in the emergence of the world of becoming. Scaliger's artist is without the restrictions of orators, philosophers, or historians, who must represent things just as they are within the world of nature. Instead, the artist has the potential to remove himself from the bounds of the divinely created world:

the poet depicts quite another sort of nature, and a variety of fortunes; in fact, by so doing, he transforms himself into a second deity. Of those things which the Maker of all framed, the other sciences are, as it were, overseers; but since poetry fashions images of those things which are not, as well as images more beautiful than life of those things which are, it seems unlike other literary forms, such as history, which confine themselves to actual events, and rather to be another god, and to create.

This glorification of the creative artist as "second deity" permeates much of Renaissance theory and criticism. It is crucial to the sculpture and sonnets of Michelangelo, the drama of Shakespeare, the political art of Machiavelli, and the art of living enunciated by Pico, More, Pomponazzi, and Vives. Unlike the architects who devised the ill-fated tower of Babel in order to become like unto God, the Renaissance architects of poetry, painting, and sculpture recognize that God has created for them another world. They are offered another haven, outside the realm of nature, in which they can safely operate without the dangers of heresy and vainglory in competing with godhead.

This world lying outside of nature, like the divine power of the artist himself, is derived from and infused with God. Yet Scaliger—like Du Bellay, Ronsard, and Sidney after him—is intent upon the use of *techné*, the regulative principles and controlling laws which the artist has at his disposal to bring order from the chaos besetting him. This is hardly the state of *entheos* that Socrates inveighs against, or the *amabilis insania* described by Horace; but then neither is it identical with the Socratic world of Pure Form. For Scaliger, invention, learning, and will lie wholly within the artist's own powers. The Deity functions only as First Cause, putting the world into being. The rest, as Machiavelli asserts, is up to man.

Much like Scaliger, Sir Philip Sidney argues in his *Apologie* that poets are distinct from astronomers, geometricians, philosophers, lawyers, historians, rhetoricians, who concern themselves only with what nature has set forth:

. . . Onely the Poet, disdayning to be tied to any such subjection, lifted up with the vigor of his owne invention, dooth growe in effect, another nature, in making things either better than Nature bringeth forth, or quite a newe formes such as never were in Nature, as the *Heroes, Demigods, Cyclops,*

*Chimeras, Furies,* and such like: so as hee goeth hand in hand with Nature, not inclosed within the narrow warrant of her guifts, but freely ranging onely within the Zodiack of his owne wit.

Stressing man's limitations as well as his potentials, Sidney argues that poetry's "final end is, to lead and draw us to as high a perfection, as our degenerate soules made worse by theyr clayey lodgings, can be capable of." Sidney's "perfection" is of this world, where man is enabled "by knowledge to lift up the mind from the dungeon of the body, to the enjoying his own divine essence." With his knowledge, his *techné*, he may range "with learned discretion into the divine consideration of what may be, and should be." Contrast the end of Sidney's art with that of Dante, "to remove those living in this life from the state of misery and lead them to the state of felicity." The felicity of Dante's medieval artist is dependent upon the perfections and powers of God's world; but with his own divine powers, Sidney's "second deity" may probe into "the sacred misteries." With his own labor, his own art, his own wit and invention, he joins those *technités* described by Pierre de Ronsard, those "happy demi-gods, they who cultivate their own earth, nor strive after another, from which they could only return thankless and unhappy, unrecompensed, and unhonored."

Keats was also to look upon art as a means of "enjoying his owne divine essence." Like Scaliger's "second deity" and Ronsard's "happy demi-gods," the nineteenth-century poet antici-

*Ltr. to Tom, 25–27 Jun. 1818*

pates being able "to add a mite to that mass of beauty which is [to be] harvested . . . and put into etherial existence" through poetry. He would "form greater things . . . than our Creator

*Ltr. to Haydon, 11 May 1817*

himself made." Not just the poetic act, but the whole of life is for Keats a process of making, of creating. But the inventions of this early nineteenth-century demi-god rise not just from learning and craft, as with Sidney and Scaliger. They rise also from the imagination and the passions. Evoked by fellow-feeling, the creative act emerges from the interaction with the things and beings which surround the artist, not just from learned discretion, the activities of a mind contemplating the world of nature and of art, those excellencies of God.

In Keats, as in most of his contemporaries, the revival of

classicism brought into question the role of *a priori* knowledge
for the creative artist. It insisted upon a different kind of
knowledge and a different kind of learning, even as it shifted
the typical Renaissance balance of capacities and limitations.
Apprehensive about the tyranny of fettered thought and limiting controls, the romantics seemed totally absorbed in exploring man's limitless capacities—that divine in every man which
Thoreau and Whitman were to invoke.

We differentiate between a theocentric Middle Ages and a
homocentric Renaissance, stressing the religious and extra-
mundane orientation of the first, the humanistic and terrestrial
preoccupation of the second. We might equally distinguish
between a homocentric Renaissance and an egocentric Romantic era, for the newer classicism of the early nineteenth century
placed an increasing emphasis upon man's unlimited potentials. Intent upon developing an egalitarian society—paradoxically, a society of strong and individualistic egos, each intent
upon achieving his own divinity—the romantics moved toward
the elevation of human worth far beyond its mundane market
value in the Middle Ages. They demanded for every man what
in the slave society of Athens had been available only for the
few.

# 4
# Classicism as Mechanism during the Age of "Reason"

For the Renaissance, the threat to felicity lurked within the imminence of fragmentation—in the disjointed and dismembered universe that threatened to disrupt, once the unity of experience and knowledge was lost. When the beast within us could no longer be reconciled with the angel, rude will with grace, foul with fair—when one could no longer "set oneself in order," as Montaigne was to suggest—then chaos ensued. Then would John Donne's prophecy be fulfilled, when the world was "all in peeces, all cohaerence gone."

In revolt against the mechanical order, firmly established by the late seventeenth and early eighteenth centuries, the romantics necessarily sought a new humanism, a new classicism from which the old values could be derived. By then, the antithesis of the celestial and the divine was no longer the brutish, the irrational, the bestial. It was the mechanical. With growing industrialism, the old fear of chaos and fragmentation had been displaced by a new fear of automation, and a distrust of mechanical laws and rigid standards, *a priori* rules and codified principles. This fear of the mechanical was for Keats and for the nineteenth century to determine a new variant of classicism, re-interpreting the principle of *techne* as the underlying determinant for learning and for the mimetic arts.

The great spokesman for the Renaissance is not a bifurcated Hamlet, alternating between being and not being, order and chaos, the philosophy at Wittenberg and the *réal politique* at Elsinore until all was indeed "in peeces." The spokesman is Shakespeare's Ulysses, an Elizabethan in Greek garb who in *Troilus and Cressida* expounds upon the dangers of this lack of "cohaerence":

> The heavens themselves, the planets, and this centre,
> Observe degree, priority, and place,
> Insisture, course, proportion, season, form,
> Office, and custom, in all line of order.
>
>                    .    .    .    .    .
>
>                          Oh, when degree is shak'd,
> Which is the ladder to all high designs,
> The enterprise is sick! How could communities,
> Degrees in schools, and brotherhoods in cities,
> Peaceful commerce from dividable shores,
> The primogenitive and due of birth,
> Prerogative of age, crowns, sceptres, laurels,
> But by degree, stand in authentic place?
> Take but degree away, untune that string,
> And hark, what discord follows! Each thing meets
> In mere oppugnancy. The bounded waters
> Should lift their bosoms higher than the shores,
> And make a sop of all this solid globe.
> Strength should be lord of imbecility,
> And the rude son should strike his father dead.
>
>                    .    .    .    .    .
>
> This chaos, when degree is suffocate,
> Follows the choking.

Order, degree, design, harmony—these were clearly the antidote for fragmentation during the Renaissance, just as for the Greeks the laws implicit in craft were the main defense against the chaos, ignorance, and discord of *barbaros*. In man's rationality to perceive order and in his freedom to correspond with this harmonious vision lay his ultimate felicity, his highest values. This is the ideal toward which both Cima and Rubens are heading with their paintings of the Endymion myth, using

ordering principles quite distinct from those at work with the ancient Greeks.

By the close of the seventeenth century, this dynamic notion of apprehending reality had solidified into a formal and self-contained doctrine, expressed by André Le Nôtre's symmetrical gardens at Versailles, in the balanced couplets of Pope, the proportioned music of Mozart, the geometric propositions of Spinoza, no less than in the mechanical structure of society and politics. For Pope, as for much of the age, the trend was directly attributable to Sir Isaac Newton:

> Nature and Nature's Laws lay hid in Night:
> GOD said, Let Newton be! and all was Light.

Voltaire was to recognize in his *Philosophical Letters* that "very few people read Newton, because it is necessary to be learned to understand him. But everybody talks about him." Newtonianism was simply in the air.

Like most of the romantics, William Blake attributed this rise of mechanization to Newton. "God forbid that Truth should be Confined to Mathematical Demonstration," Blake had exclaimed in his annotations to Reynolds' *Discourses,* cautioning that "the End of Epicurean or Newtonian Philosophy . . . is Atheism."

> The Atoms of Democritus
> And Newton's Particles of light
> Are sands upon the Red sea shore,
> Where Israel's tents do shine so bright.

Keats shared these same apprehensions about Newtonianism. Haydon records that at his "immortal dinner," during the Christmas week of 1817, Keats joined with Lamb in agreeing that Newton "had destroyed all the poetry of the rainbow by reducing it to the prismatic colours." With this, the whole company, including Wordsworth, drank a toast to "Newton's health, and confusion to mathematics."

Blake, Lamb, and Keats were not far wrong. The author of the *Principia* had portrayed the universe as a single, vast, and

uniform mechanism, whose every event could be mathematically deduced from the fundamental principles of its mechanical action. Whereas the medievalists had unfolded a *mysterium*, inaccessible to the human mind, but with an ascending hierarchy of increasingly hidden divine purposes, Newton's universe was projected as a uniform system, subject to a single known law. Its basis was not in Aristotelean syllogistic logic, but in Euclidean geometry.

Earlier, Spinoza had dealt in his *Ethics* with man and God through a series of definitions, axioms, corollaries, and propositions, as if they were part of a geometric system. And later, Alexander Pope, somewhat imitative of Newtonian uniformitarianism, was to offer a perfection of the closed heroic couplet in his *Essay on Man,* where a symmetry of poetic form corresponds with the symmetry of world order—a balance of word against word, stress against stress, phrase against phrase, line against line, image against image, idea against idea. Similarly, Sir William Temple, carrying Newtonian principles into horticulture, had upheld as "the perfectest figure of a garden I ever saw," the geometric gardens of Moor Park, where "beauty of building and planting is placed chiefly in some certain proportions, symmetrie, or uniformitie; our walls and our trees ranged so as to answer one another, and at exact distances."

According to Keats, Newton shares with Boileau this responsibility for destroying "the poetry of the rainbow." Under Boileau, craftsmen of the prior age had developed a schism, confusing artifice for beauty, mechanical art for true creativity. Nurtured alike by barbarism and foppery,

> with a puling infant's force
> They sway'd about upon a rocking horse,
> And thought it Pegasus.

SLEEP AND POETRY,
*185–206*

Under Boileau, the cult of Pegasus and Apollo was dead:

> A thousand handicraftsmen wore the mask
> Of Poesy. Ill-fated, impious race!
> That blasphemed the bright Lyrist to his face,
> And did not know it,—no, they went about,

> Holding a poor, decrepid standard out
> Mark'd with most flimsy mottos, and in large
> The name of one Boileau!

Guided by the influential author of *L'Art Poétique,* this
"school of dolts" confused poetry with artifice and mathematical contrivance.

Although Keats may tend to confuse the nature and intent of
Boileau's standards, an examination of *L'Art Poétique* reveals
the source of some of his apprehensions. In conformity with
contemporary laws of decorum, reason, and symmetry, Boileau
was instrumental in setting up a fairly rigid code for poetry.
Easily attributable to classical principles enunciated by Aristotle and filtered through Horace and Lope de Vega, this code
is actually no closer to the dynamics of Periclean Athens than
Aquinas' medieval interpretation of Aristotle or Scaliger's Renaissance variant. These all represent deviations from classicism,
and reserving the term "neo-classical" for Boileau and his followers is highly misleading. This late seventeenth-century code
is implicit in an Horatian statement of taste expressed in
Boileau's initial canto:

> More pleased we are to see a river lead
> His gentle streams along a flowery mead
> Than from high banks to hear loud torrents roar,
> With foamy waters on a muddy shore. . . .
> Each object must be fixed in the due place,
> And differing parts have corresponding grace;
> Till by a curious art disposed, we find
> One perfect whole, of all the pieces joined.

Boileau's world of nature seemingly embraces both harmony
and discord, both "gentle streams" and "loud torrents." But the
world of external nature is not to be confused by the artist with
what he ought to represent through his art. In joining together
"all the pieces," he must fix "each object . . . in the due place."
The painter or poet must wend his stream "along a flowery
mead," and never along "a muddy shore." In striving for the
"one perfect whole," he is ruled by reason and judgment. He

orders his materials, but not to reveal the potentiality of muddy shores within the world of matter, nor even to provide a harmony of terrestrial discord and heavenly concord. He would emulate the ideal: the order, harmony, proportion, symmetry implicit in the perfection of the Deity. To imitate external Nature, its unity *and* its diversity—in politics, as in art—is to pursue the bestial, the corrupt, the sinful, the irrational, as Boileau makes clear before the close of his poem:

> Before kind reason did her light display,
> And government taught mortals to obey,
> Men, like wild beasts, did nature's laws pursue,
> They fed on herbs, and drink from rivers drew:
> Might held sway, instead of right and rule.

Political and artistic liberty in Boileau is not to be confused with nineteenth-century egalitarianism. True "liberty" is more Horatian freedom to follow the just, the proper, the rational, the established rules—and not, as with Keats, the freedom to pursue the dizzied flights of the imagination and the surgings of passion which are alone at the core of social sympathy and brotherhood. And "proper" is not to be found, as with the author of *Lamia,* within

> 　　　　　a gordian shape of dazzling hue,　　　　LAMIA, *I, 47–53*
> Vermilion-spotted, golden, green, and blue;
> Striped like a zebra, freckled like a pard,
> Eyed like a peacock, and all crimson barr'd;
> And full of silver moons, that, as she breathed,
> Dissolv'd, or brighter shone, or interwreathed
> Their lustres with the gloomier tapestries . . .

For Boileau, "proper" is to be discerned only in the light of "kind reason" and through "curious [*viz.,* precise] art," those mainstays of ideal nature for the late seventeenth century.

The principle of unity, the "one perfect whole" that Boileau would find in art as in nature, is clearly inconsonant with Aristotelean organicism. For Aristotle, unity of plot had been dependent upon the laws of potency, the function of the artist

being to relate what may happen, to assist in bringing into being what is possible according to the laws of probability or necessity, the potentialities of form emergent from matter. The possibilities of Hector are not the possibilities of Achilles; a *media via* possible for Milo the wrestler is different in kind from that of the poet. In the *Poetics* and in the *Ethics*, Aristotle is working within a different world of forms, one more consonant with that of Sophocles, than of either Boileau or Keats.

Boileau's "neo-classical" assumptions may not be in strict accord with those of Aristotle or Sophocles, but they are fairly consonant with Thomas Burnet's in *The Sacred Theory of the Earth*, where Burnet distinguishes nature as she now is and as she must have emerged originally from the hands of a perfect and rational Creator. In its initial form, nature was orderly, symmetrical, rational, regular—one eternal spring. In its present post-diluvian form, she is disorderly, irrational, irregular. But her present form is no reflection of her Maker, Burnet explains:

We think him a better Artist that makes a Clock that strikes regularly at every hour from the Springs and Wheels which he puts in the work, than he that hath so made his Clock that he must put his finger to it every hour to make it strike: And if one should contrive a piece of Clock-work so that it should beat all the hours, and make its motions regularly for such a time, and that time being come, upon a signal given, or a Spring toucht, it should of its own accord fall all to pieces; would not this be look'd upon as a piece of greater Art, than if the Workman came at that time prefixt, and with a great Hammer beat it to pieces? I use these comparisons to convince us that it is no detraction from Divine Providence, that the course of Nature is exact and regular, and that even in its greatest changes and revolutions it should still conspire and be prepar'd to answer the ends and purposes of the Divine Will in reference to the Moral World.

If we would anticipate any return to the original state of perfection, then this must be through imitation of the exactness and regularity of Nature in her original form.

Burnet's account may seem grossly implausible to us, but given assumptions of the late seventeenth century, he was not to be ignored. "Of our present sea, rocks, mountains, etc., I think you have given the most plausible account," Newton commented in a letter to Burnet (*c.* 1681) . "I write not to oppose

you, for I think the main part of your hypothesis as probable as that I have here written, if not in some respects more probable."

"The Great Design of Arte is to restore the Decays that happen'd to human Nature by the Fall, by restoring Order," John Dennis was to write in *The Grounds of Criticism.* And similar assumptions are to be found in *The Idea of Painting, Sculpture and Architecture,* a discourse read in May, 1664, before the Academy of St. Luke at Rome by Giovanni Pietro Bellori. Enjoining the painter to imitate only the regularities of a rational and perfect Maker, Bellori cautions against any representation of the grossness and deformity of nature as she confronts us in this mutable sublunary sphere:

. . . The artful painter and sculptor, imitating the Divine Maker, form to themselves, as well as they are able, a model of the superior beauties; and reflecting on them, endeavour to correct and amend the common nature, and to represent it as it was at first created, without fault, either in colour, or in lineament.

Bellori's "Divine Maker"—the Supreme Architect and Heavenly Designer—is far removed from the Omnibenevolent Deity projected by William Paley in the early nineteenth century as a God of unlimited sympathy and love. But Bellori shares in the classical world of forms inherent for Boileau, Burnet, and Dennis. And his assumptions are basic to the allegorical interpretation of Endymion offered by Alexander Ross in his *Mystagogus Poeticus:*

By *Endymeon Adam* may be meant, who was faire whilest Gods image continued with him; but when he fell in love with *Juno, Jupiters wife,* that is affected equality with his Maker, he was thrust out of Paradise into this world, as into a cave, where he was cast into a dead sleep, or the sleep of death, from which he shall not be awaked, though the Moon so often visit him; that is, so long as the Moon shall shine and visit the earth (which shall be till the dissolution of all things) man shall sleep in the grave. . . . When *Endymeon,* that is, man-kind slept in sin, the Moon, that is, our Saviour Christ (whose flesh is compared to the Moon (in Psal. 73) by S. *Augustine,* as his divinitie to the Sun) in his flesh visited us, and dwelt amongst us; this Moon was eclipsed in the passion, and this Moon slept in the cave with *Adam,* and the full of this Moon was seen in the resurrection. . . .

The myth of Endymion, as interpreted by Ross, seems to
share less in the inheritance of Ovid or John Lyly, and more in
the abhorrence of jagged rocks and waterfalls, mountains and
torrents, so basic to late seventeenth-century concepts of disorder and imperfection. Like Keats's own interpretation, that of
Ross is obviously predicated upon a system of classical values
both inherent in and divorced from the values of Periclean
Athens. But the classical myth emerging from Ross is more
Christian than pagan; more seventeenth-century than Greek.
Its organizing principles are shared more by Milton and Bun-
yan, Boileau and Dryden, than by Plato and Aristotle. It partakes more of the "rational" principles of Poussin who would
contrast the serenity of a divine Selene with the wild distrac-
tions of a mortal Endymion. Order arises from disorder;
unity, from multiplicity and variety.

With an analogous view of craft, Henry Fielding offers *Tom
Jones* and *Joseph Andrews,* not as new inventions, but as comic-
epic poems in prose, imitations or re-discoveries of pre-existent forms. Boileau and Dryden offer satires and epistles in
imitation of Juvenal and Horace. Corneille and Racine affect
art mimetic of the classical theater. And Rapin and Pope
produce pastorals in imitation of Theocritus and an earlier
golden age. But the imitations are never wholly mimetic; they
offer always a re-interpretation and a re-assimilation of older
materials and more ancient methods, as with Keats's handling
of Endymion.

Understandably, when the myth of Endymion appears in
poetry or painting of the Age of "Reason," its artistic principles
emanate out of assumptions about an age of innocence, when
man was first emerging from the hand of his Maker: simple,
happy, humble, bucolic—the ideal toward which even the
French aristocracy under Louis XVI strove, *jouer a bergère,*
playing the shepherd's game in the gardens of Versailles, with
perfumed cows and noble dairy maids. If we would copy nature, Alexander Pope suggests in his *Discourse on Pastoral
Poetry,* then "we are not to describe our shepherds as shepherds
at this day really are, but as they may be conceived then to have
been; when the best of men followed the employment." Pur-
portedly following the classical practice of Theocritus and Vir-

gil, Pope urges that to render a pastoral delightful "consists in exposing the best side only of a shepherd's life, and in concealing its miseries." Not nature in all her discords, but nature improved and dressed to advantage, becomes the object of imitation, the basis of *techné*. The task of the "neo-classical" craftsman is to know nature—as she is, but also as she once was, and as she still strives to be:

> Unerring Nature, still divinely bright,
> One clear, unchanged, and universal light,
> Life, force, and beauty must to all impart,
> At once the source and end, and test of Art.

For this kind of classicist, *techné* may involve various kinds of knowledge and various principles of ordering—but inevitably it gravitates about an epistemological and conceptualizing core. It aims at felicity, but not without the directions afforded by learning, by understanding, by knowledge and technique.

Keats and the newer classicists seemed to move in direct opposition to this age-old tradition of *techné,* in search of a highly individualistic art, a creative process free of superimposed rules, restricted systems, and inherited ideas. The newer classicism was to be dependent, not upon a conceptualized world of pre-existent forms, but upon a perceptual world of things with which man might interact. In *Jerusalem,* Blake was to explain this movement with the words of Los:

> I must Create a System or be enslav'd by another Man's.
> I will not Reason & Compare: my business is to Create.

# The Keatsian Poetic

"I must Create a System
  or be enslav'd by another Man's.
I will not Reason & Compare:
my business is to Create."
So Los in fury & strength,
in indignation & burning wrath.
—William Blake, *Jerusalem* (X)

# 5

# The Grand Materials of
# Creativity: The Vale
# of Soul-Making

Late in 1817 Keats was busily completing his draft of *Endymion*. Dimly and incoherently, he was fumbling for a poetical system, and the lengthy narrative poem was yet to be envisioned as some kind of aesthetic whole. For several weeks in September, Keats had visited with Benjamin Bailey at his Magdalen Hall quarters in Oxford. He was working with some regularity and ease on the third book of *Endymion,* while Bailey, who had matriculated at Oxford the previous year, was reading for holy orders. Shortly after the friends separated, Bailey's hopes for a curacy seemed momentarily to have been thwarted. When he heard the news, the twenty-two year old Keats sat down, as much to vent his adolescent spleen against this "unlook'd for piece of villainy," as to lament his failure at offering any kind of real consolation. He wrote to Bailey: "O for a recourse somewhat human independant of the great Consolations of Religion and undepraved Sensations—of the Beautiful—the poetical in all things—O for a Remedy against such wrongs within the pale of the World!" For Bailey, about to take holy orders, this must have appeared as curious consolation—though Bailey must have known about the poet's a-religious stance. Much later, Bailey was to note in one of his letters

*Ltr. to Bailey,*
*3 Nov. 1817*

that Keats had even at this early stage been approaching the "abominable principles" of Shelley, that sensual love is at the root of things. And Haydon flattered himself into thinking that Keats "had a tendency to Christianity when he first knew [me]; & Hunt soon forced his tendencies in another direction."

Keats's search is for a "human" recourse, independent of religion. Typically, his concern here is with "the Beautiful—the poetical in all things," those *things* which lie "within the pale of the World." This was indeed a search destined to plague the poet for the whole of his existence, dependent as it was upon "the yearning Passion I have for the beautiful." It permeates his earlier verse and letters, as well as the later. This was the daemon that pushed him on to discover a remedy for worldly suffering with things that lie, not beyond, but *within* this earthly pale.

*Ltr. to George &*
*Georgiana,*
*24 Oct. 1818*

By the spring of 1819, Keats found his "Remedy"—though as always, cosmology and aesthetics are so closely interwoven for him as to be almost indistinguishable. In the earlier letter of 1817, he had expressed to Bailey only an inchoate longing, an inarticulate wish. Within a year and a half, the remedy is developed at length and with decisiveness in a journal-letter to George and Georgiana. His elder brother had emigrated with his wife in the summer of 1818 to America, and the lengthy letters forwarded to them by Keats are among the most revealing in his correspondence. At times, vocabulary and syntax are curious and confusing in this 1819 letter, but the meaning is relatively lucid. The angry frustration bursting through the earlier letter to Bailey is here displaced by a mind straining with the immensity of an idea. By the middle of 1819, the rosebud had unfolded. The man who was writing the *Ode on a Grecian Urn* had emerged from the youth who had been responsible for *Endymion:*

*Ltr. to George &*
*Georgiana,*
*21 Apr. 1819*

The common cognomen of this world among the misguided and superstitious is 'a vale of tears' from which we are to be redeemed by a certain arbitrary interposition of God and taken to Heaven—What a little circumscribed straightened notion! Call the world if you Please "The vale of Soul-making" Then you will find out the use of the world (I am speaking now in the highest terms for human nature admitting it to be immortal which I will here take for granted for the purpose of showing a thought

which has struck me concerning it) I say 'Soul making' Soul as distinguished from an Intelligence—There may be intelligences or sparks of the
divinity in millions—but they are not Souls till they acquire identities, till
each one is personally itself. Intelligences are atoms of perception—they
know and they see and they are pure, in short they are God—how then are
Souls to be made? How then are these sparks which are God to have
identity given them—so as ever to possess a bliss peculiar to each ones
individual existence? How, but by the medium of a world like this? This
point I sincerely wish to consider because I think it a grander system of
salvation than the chrystain religion—or rather it is a system of Spirit-creation—This is effected by three grand materials acting the one upon the
other for a series of years—These three Materials are the *Intelligence*—the
*human heart* (as distinguished from intelligence or Mind) and the *World*
or *Elemental space* suited for the proper action of *Mind and Heart* on
each other for the purpose of forming the *Soul* or *Intelligence destined to
possess the sense of Identity*. I can scarcely express what I but dimly
perceive—and yet I think I perceive it. . . . As various as the Lives of Men
are—so various become their souls, and thus does God make individual
beings, Souls, Identical Souls of the sparks of his own essence—This
appears to me a faint sketch of a system of Salvation which does not affront
our reason and humanity. . . .

This "system of Salvation" is called alternately by Keats "a
system of Spirit-creation" or a "System of Soul-making." It is
offered as "a grander system . . . than the chrystain religion."
  In this 1819 letter Keats, like the late seventeenth-century
metaphysician Leibniz, envisions divine creativity as a fulgura-
tion from a single and central source by which "intelligences or
sparks of the divinity in millions" come into being, "Identical
Souls of the Sparks of his own essence." Leibniz had concentrated in his *Monadology*, however, upon the continuous creative process of an absolutely perfect divinity, one whose perfection and wisdom can be recognized in the mechanical structure
of particular bodies. For Leibniz, every organism is "a kind of
divine machine or natural automaton," mechanical unto its
smallest living parts, distinct from the mechanical but non-liv-
ing creations of man's art. Inasmuch as man, like all else in His
creation, is only "sparked off" the Divine Being, he is necessarily less than God and can participate only to a limited extent in
His perfection. But for Keats, as distinct from the mechanistic
and theocentric Leibniz, a second and much more significant
creation takes place through man's artistry: the process of

"soul-making" by which man moulds his own individual identity. More in keeping with many of his contemporaries who
sought during the early nineteenth century a revival of the
humanistic principles of ancient Greece, Keats is intent upon
stressing man's potential rather than his limitations; a mortal's
creative capacity, rather than God's; the human ability to forge
the beautiful and poetical from all the things within the pale of
this world. His directions are recognizably Greek and Platonic.

According to Keats's vision, the divine creator puts into
being "three grand materials" which act upon one another for
a series of years. One is *"Intelligence"*—the mind with its
ability to know, to discern, to analyze, to philosophize. This is
the *cogito* of Descartes, and Keats suggests that Coleridge and
Wordsworth had this quality in excess. But intelligence is to be
distinguished from the second grand material, that seat of
man's passions, the "human heart," which has the capacity to
"feel and suffer in a thousand diverse ways." These two materials—*"Intelligence"* and *"the human heart"*—seem encompassed within yet a third, "the *World* or *Elemental space* suited
for the proper action of *Mind and Heart* on each other." Man's
creation of his own soul is presumably effected by these three
materials acting upon one another for a series of years. In the
case of little children, whose intelligence has had no time to be
altered by the heart, the spark returns upon death to its source
without any identity; but with men who have had the time for
provings and testings, perfectionings and alterations, "the sense
of Identity" can be made. How?—"through the medium of the
Heart. And how is the heart to become this Medium but in a
world of Circumstances?"

Man is assigned the task of making his own identity. In the
creative process, as soul-maker, man is offered a role which can
serve as an antidote to the common and misguided notion that
he can be redeemed from this "vale of tears" only through the
arbitrary intervention of an anthropomorphic Being. This misguided notion, Keats insists, can only affront our humanity and
our reason. Because this is a vale of soul-making, rather than a
vale of tears, man should face life as well as death with the
greatest equanimity.

Keatsian equanimity is far removed from the universal peace

and harmonious order that Dryden had anticipated in *Religio Laici* or Pope in his *Epistle to Dr. Arbuthnot*. But then, the "world of Circumstances" or "Elemental space" which Keats projects is hardly the rational and geometric universe of the late seventeenth and early eighteenth centuries. Then, a *plenum formarum*—symmetrical, proportioned, balanced— had been envisioned as God's design. Leibniz had considered the Deity "as the architect of the mechanism of the world," the efficient cause of our being. For Leibniz, the Divinity "does nothing which is not orderly, and . . . it is not even possible to conceive of events which are not regular." Rational and geometric, the all-perfect Master Architect had of necessity created the best of all possible worlds: with continuity, plenitude, and gradation.

In his *Essay on Man*, Alexander Pope had expatiated

> o'er all this scene of Man;
> A mighty maze! but not without a plan,

a maze revealing strong connections, precise dependencies, and just gradations. Here, within this vast scale of being, all that rises must ascend in due degree. Before too many decades, Voltaire was to scoff at the patent absurdities of this "best of all possible worlds," while common-sense Samuel Johnson found himself entertained but not particularly enlightened by this doctrine to which humanity, no less than its Maker, was unequal. By the turn of that century, the static chain was to become transformed into a ladder of ascent. "All things strive to ascend, and ascend in their striving. And shall man alone stoop?" Coleridge was to ask in one of his *Aphorisms*. But for the earlier era, Pope's description was apt and acceptable:

> Vast chain of Being! which from God began,
> Natures ethereal, human, angel, man,
> Beast, bird, fish, insect, what no eye can see,
> No glass can reach; from Infinite to thee,
> From thee to nothing.—On superior powers
> Were we to press, inferior might on ours:
> Or in the full creation leave a void,

Where, one step broken, the great scale's destroyed:
From Nature's chain whatever link you strike,
Tenth or ten thousandth breaks the chain alike.

In this vast chain of being, partial evil is but universal good; human suffering, derived from nature or from man—plagues or earthquakes, a Catiline or a Borgia—exists as part of heaven's larger design. Pains and annoyances, perceptible to man's limited vision, form part of the larger order, in which to reason rightly is to submit. Whatever is, Pope urges, must be right. Human will must properly be subordinated to the greater design, the peace and order of Divine Harmony. We may recognize this design—manifest in Pope, in Dryden, in Leibniz—as a logic and order peculiar to neo-classicism of the late seventeenth and early eighteenth centuries; but it seems quite inappropriate to recognize it as the only variant of classicism.

Keats's emphasis is never upon God's rational and ordering capacity, no more than it rests upon His original design, wherein human suffering is stoically accepted as part of an invisible symmetry. On the contrary, for Keats a "World of Pains and troubles is [necessary] to school an Intelligence and make it a soul." The irrational brutality of the present can be diminished—but not by conformity to the rationale of the past, the restoration of an Edenic state created by God prior to man's fall. Nor is it diminished by conformity to a future which has been pre-determined by a Will external to that of man. Keats is appalled by the common Christian idea of salvation: "I do not at all believe in this sort of perfectibility—the nature of the world will not admit of it—the inhabitants of the world will correspond to itself." Pains and annoyances are as native to this vale as existence itself. Decay is a process that must inevitably follow fruition, the autumnal dirge that must follow upon the songs of spring, the pain that must ever attend bliss. Suppose a rose to have sensation, he suggests. On a beautiful morning, it blooms, it enjoys itself. But then there comes a cold wind or a hot sun. It cannot escape these; it cannot destroy these annoyances, for they are as native to the world as the rose itself—and "no more can man be happy in spite, the worldly elements will prey upon his nature."

*Ltr. to George &*
*Georgiana,*
*21 Apr. 1819*

Every thing is spoilt by use:                    FANCY, *68–73*
Where's the cheek that doth not fade,
Too much gaz'd at? Where's the maid
Whose lip mature is ever new?
Where's the eye, however blue,
Doth not weary?

The great odes, emerging from the same period as this April, 1819 section of the journal-letter, reflect this "World of Pains and troubles." This human condition, this state of "breathing human passion," is one in which man must expect "a heart high-sorrowful and cloy'd, / A burning forehead, and a parching tongue." This is a "sweet and bitter world" in which bitterness is as indigenous as sweetness. The creative poet and the maker of souls are working through the tears and with the bitterness, rather than struggling to get beyond them into a Christian Heaven or a Platonic world of Pure Form. There may be a desperate longing to fade and dissolve with the nightingale, much as Shelley longs for the harmonious madness of the skylark, and Wordsworth with his cuckoo must transform the world into "an unsubstantial faery place." But always, with Keats, there is for mortal man an essential need for reconciliation with

ODE ON A
GRECIAN URN, *III*

LINES WRITTEN IN
THE HIGHLANDS, *30*

The weariness, the fever, and the fret                ODE TO A
  Here, where men sit and hear each other groan;        NIGHTINGALE, *III*
Where palsy shakes a few, sad, last gray hairs,
  Where youth grows pale, and spectre-thin, and dies;
    Where but to think is to be full of sorrow
      And leaden-eyed despairs,
  Where Beauty cannot keep her lustrous eyes,
    Or new Love pine at them beyond to-morrow.

To be tasted, Joy's grape must be devoured. The strenuous tongue must burst the very source of its delight. The act of life, like the act of love, is potentially an act of annihilation. There is with Keats the recognition that "in the very temple of Delight / Veil'd Melancholy has her sovran shrine." Think not with regret upon the passing of "the songs of Spring"; delight,

ODE ON
MELANCHOLY, *III*

TO AUTUMN, *III*

rather, in the music of mourning and the soft-dying day. The whole system of soul-making appears to resolve itself into this:

*Ltr. to George &
Georgiana,
21 Apr. 1819*—that Man is originally 'a poor forked creature' subject to the same mischances as the beasts of the forest, destined to hardships and disquietude of some kind or other. If he improves by degrees his bodily accomodations and comforts—at each stage, at each ascent there are waiting for him a fresh set of annoyances—he is mortal and there is still a heaven with its Stars above his head.

Having offered his disquisition on the "vale of Soul-making," Keats then proceeds to transform the system into "the most homely form possible" for George and Georgiana:

I will call the *world* a School instituted for the purpose of teaching little children to read—I will call the *human heart* the *horn Book* used in that School—and I will call the *Child able to read, the Soul* made from that *school* and its *hornbook.* Do you not see how necessary a World of Pains and troubles is to school an Intelligence and make it a soul? A Place where the heart must feel and suffer in a thousand diverse ways! Not merely is the Heart a Hornbook, It is the Minds Bible, it is the Minds experience, it is the teat from which the Mind or intelligence sucks its identity. . . .

Divinity may be responsible for the three grand materials— the intelligence, the heart, and elemental space—which are to act and react upon one another. Yet in typical classical fashion, the task of directing the action and forming his own identity falls upon man himself. Keats would find his identity, not through the balance or order or symmetry, so crucial to Pope; not through the weighing and numbering and measuring, so vital to Defoe's characters in search of their identity. In Keats, man "sucks" his identity from a worldly "teat." The experience is sensorial, as well as cognitive. It is erotic and pleasure-seeking, as well as creative.

Regardless of pain or pleasure, the three materials are both necessary and acceptable, if only because they make possible man's creation of a fourth material. To the six days reserved for creation in *Genesis,* Keats adds a seventh. This seventh day consumes the entirety of every man's lifetime. While Divinity
*Ltr. to Haydon,
11 May 1817*rests, the new creator must proceed with his alloted task, "looking upon the Sun the Moon the Stars, the Earth and its contents

as materials to form greater things—that is to say ethereal things—but here I am talking like a Madman," Keats exclaims to the artist Benjamin Robert Haydon, "—greater things than our Creator himself made!!" In expressing to his brother Tom his fascination for the mountains and waterfalls in the Lake district, Keats is consumed by the same mad thought. He *Ltr. to Tom, 25–27 Jun. 1818* trembles with anticipation at "being able to add a mite to that mass of beauty which is harvested from these grand materials, by the finest spirits, and put into etherial existence for the relish of one's fellows."

Man's task in creating his own identity, then, is "to add a mite to that mass of beauty." He must form "greater things than our Creator himself made." He sets out "to school an Intelligence and make it a Soul." But this is also, and simultaneously, the task of man struggling to create poetry, for the creation of poetry is part of the soul-making process. Poetry-making is a means, though not the only means, of forging one's identity. Through music, friendship, love, as the poet tells us everywhere, we may also find the means for creating our souls, providing

> the leaven,
> That spreading in this dull and clodded earth
> Gives it a touch ethereal—a new birth . . .

*ENDYMION, I, 296–8*

Indeed, in its seeming all-inclusiveness, life itself, the whole of life, experienced in its fullness, offers material for the creative process: the songs of Spring, but also the wailful choir of Autumn; the temple of Delight, as well as the sovereign shrine of Melancholy; the rose full-blown, but also the rose destroyed. Nothing is denied the new creator. Nothing is omitted from the workshop of a world. With typical egalitarianism, Keats makes this a craft and a workshop available to everyone alike. Whereas Wordsworth and Shelley were denying differences of kind between the poet and other men, even while stressing differences of degree in sensibility, Keats makes no such refinement. Instead, he seems to give ready approval to Hazlitt's insistence that "Man is a poetical animal: and those of us who do not study the principles of poetry, act upon them all our

lives, like Molière's Bourgeois Gentilhomme, who had always spoken prose without knowing it."

We are all potential creators, and the materials or objects of our creativity are all-inclusive, the artist having at his disposal the bitter and the sweet; the painful and the pleasurable; the real and the imaginary; the valuable and the insignificant. The "three grand materials" act upon one another for a series of years: the material and substantive in Elemental Space ("the Sun the Moon the Stars, the Earth and its contents"), but simultaneously human hearts and minds. In creating his soul or identity, man must direct his concern toward this interaction, the process, the experience, rather than towards objects, goals, events, or ideas. If the aesthetic process is said to be mimetic, it must necessarily for Keats be an imitation of that interaction, and not a representation of intellectual ideas or corporeal things or historical events. As a second divinity, the poet essays to "put into etherial existence" those grand materials already created by his divine predecessor.

Distinct from the *poiêtês* or maker of the Renaissance, that "second deity" who differed from other men by virtue of his knowledge, a craft that enabled him to invent another world outside the realm of nature, Keats's artist can create with little knowledge; "if Poetry comes not as naturally as the Leaves to a tree it had better not come at all." Like Hazlitt's poetical animal and Molière's *gentilhomme,* he needs little learning to perform the natural and instinctive. Creativity for this "second deity" rises not from any pre-conceived knowledge of the world of nature, but from an interaction with that world, an experience with it.

*Ltr. to Taylor, 27 Feb. 1818*

The "vale of Soul-making" letter had tried to explain, from a cosmogonical perspective, the origin of the soul, the source of man's identity. A year before, Keats had struggled from yet another perspective with the system of values inherent in the creative process:

*Ltr. to Bailey, 13 Mar. 1818*

As Tradesmen say every thing is worth what it will fetch, so probably every mental pursuit takes its reality and worth from the ardour of the pursuer —being in itself a nothing—Ethereal things may at least be thus real, divided into three heads—Things real—things semireal—and no things— Things real—such as existences of Sun Moon & Stars and passages of Shakspeare—Things semireal such as Love, the Clouds &c which require

a greeting of the Spirit to make them wholly exist—and Nothings which
are made Great and dignified by an ardent pursuit. . . .

How can man, as artist, as creator, make the things of this
world dignified and great?—this is the problem confronting
Keats here. Turned inside out, this same problem is posed in
the "vale of Soul-making" letter—how can the second creator
forge his soul, his identity?

Through the "ardour of the pursuer" who is intent on creating his identity, the no things of the world—the smallest gnat, a
fading violet, a coffin worm, a meagre face deformed—can
assume significance and value. They can be "made Great and
dignified by an ardent pursuit." Reversing the Greek maxim
—*ex nihilo nihilo fit,* nothing comes of nothing—Keats is insistent that something can indeed come from nothing. Deliberately, ardently, heart interacts with mind in pursuit of the
things in elemental space: (1) "things real," including divinely
created materials ("Sun Moon & Stars"), but also man-made
materials ("Passages of Shakspeare"); (2) "things semireal,"
including the clouds created by divinity, as well as the love
produced by mortals; and (3) "no things." There is apparently
nothing (or "no thing") that has not the power within this
world of pains and troubles to make of man's mortal being an
immortality.

Keats's direction with this hierarchical pursuit of "no
things," to give them dignity and worth, is quite the reverse of
that undertaken by Leontes in Shakespeare's *The Winter's
Tale.* For Leontes, faithfulness in marriage and in friendship
seems the only viable reality, but he confuses appearances with
reality, "things real" with "no things."

> Is whispering nothing?
> Is leaning cheek to cheek? Is meeting noses?
> Kissing with inside lip? Stopping the career
> Of laughter with a sigh—a note infallible
> Of breaking honesty?—Horsing foot on foot?
> Skulking in corners? Wishing clocks more swift?
> Hours, minutes? Noon, midnight? And all eyes
> Blind with the pin and web but theirs, theirs only,
> That would unseen be wicked? Is this nothing?

> Why, then the world and all that's in 't is nothing,
> The covering sky is nothing, Bohemia's nothing,
> My wife is nothing, nor nothing have these nothings
> If this be nothing.

Confronted throughout the drama with the appearance of deceit, Leontes proceeds to reduce everything to nothing, to diminish reality and worth. He proves destructive and malicious, quite the opposite of Keats whose creativity would dote on all nothings that he might make of them a something, adding his mite to existence.

Despite this seeming all-inclusiveness, Keats is hardly indiscriminate in his total embrace of all things and all experiences as materials for the creative act. A hierarchy of values implicit in this letter to Bailey seems to indicate that though nothings can be made great and dignified by an ardent pursuit, a diminution of ardor can lessen their greatness and dignity, their reality and worth. Materials or objects confronting the artist can in varying degrees be real or unreal, worthy or unworthy, great or insignificant—but values are derived "from the ardour of the pursuer." These are materials as well as values, consecrated not to God, but to ourselves, to our own immortality. The ardent pursuer strives to dissolve the isolating boundaries between things and self, the hardened core that would prevent the formulation of his own identity:

*Ltr. to Bailey,*
*13 Mar. 1818*

> [Man] chews the honied cud of fair spring thoughts,
> Till, in his Soul dissolv'd they come to be
> Part of himself.

But then, if we are not to proceed contrary to Keats's aesthetic, it is important, as the poet himself cautions, not to wed ourselves "To musty laws lined out with wretched rule / And compass vile," smoothing, clipping, and fitting, until letter and verse tally. One must with Keats somehow tease the spirit out of thought which only clips the wings and empties the haunted air. To experience for ourselves these materials of elemental space, or to pursue with Keats his own intensive ardor, should prove much more illuminating than any dialectical discussion of these grand materials and their interaction.

SLEEP AND POETRY,
*195–9*

LAMIA,
*II, 234–6*

# 6

# The Grand Materials of Creativity: Things and No Things

The hierarchy of values at work with Keats is perhaps nowhere more apparent than in two passages of *Endymion*, both crucial to an unraveling of this lengthy poem. Frequently dismissed as a poetic failure, an adolescent trial, prolix and disorganized, *Endymion* contains two passages crucial to Keats's assumptions during this early date about the poetic materials at his disposal. As always, theory must be an echo of the practice for the poet.

The first passage is the thirty-five line introductory section, appropriately introducing the theme of the larger drama. The second, Endymion's speech to Peona on the nature of happiness (I, 769–842), outlines the structural development of that theme. Significantly, Keats himself refers to his revision of the latter passage as being "of the greatest Service to me of any thing I ever did." *Ltr. to Taylor, 30 Jan. 1818*

A THING of beauty is a joy for ever:  *ENDYMION, I, 1–35*
Its loveliness increases; it will never
Pass into nothingness; but still will keep
A bower quiet for us, and a sleep
Full of sweet dreams, and health, and quiet breathing.

Therefore, on every morrow, are we wreathing
A flowery band to bind us to the earth,
Spite of despondence, of the inhuman dearth
Of noble natures, of the gloomy days,
Of all the unhealthy and o'er-darkened ways
Made for our searching: yes, in spite of all,
Some shape of beauty moves away the pall
From our dark spirits. Such the sun, the moon,
Trees old, and young sprouting a shady boon
For simple sheep; and such are daffodils
With the green world they live in; and clear rills
That for themselves a cooling covert make
'Gainst the hot season; the mid forest brake,
Rich with a sprinkling of fair musk-rose blooms:
And such too is the grandeur of the dooms
We have imagined for the mighty dead;
All lovely tales that we have heard or read:
An endless fountain of immortal drink,
Pouring unto us from the heaven's brink.

Nor do we merely feel these essences
For one short hour; no, even as the trees
That whisper round a temple become soon
Dear as the temple's self, so does the moon,
The passion poesy, glories infinite,
Haunt us till they become a cheering light
Unto our souls, and bound to us so fast,
That, whether there be shine, or gloom o'ercast,
They alway must be with us, or we die.

Therefore, 'tis with full happiness that I
Will trace the story of Endymion.

Like the closing couplet in the *Ode on a Grecian Urn*, the opening lines of *Endymion* have generally been glossed as a romantic aphorism or seized upon as a liturgical truth. Critics have puzzled over the final lines of the *Grecian Urn*, but few have paused over this passage of *Endymion*. Almost invariably, the initial lines are interpreted as a manifesto about the eter-

nality of beauty. And yet, the syntactical subordination of *beauty* to THING in the first line would seem to stress the corporeality of beauty, rather than its abstracted quality. For Keats, beauty resides in the quantitative world of things, substantive and material. In man's love there is nestled a kernel,

LINES ON SEEING
A LOCK OF
MILTON'S HAIR

> the kernel of . . . earthly love,
> Beauty, in things on earth, and things above.

Ltr. to George &
Georgiana,
24 Oct. 1818

With Keats's "mighty abstract Idea . . . of Beauty," the abstraction is "of Beauty in all things." To Fanny Brawne, Keats offers a similar assurance that he has always "lov'd the principle of beauty in all things." This is a concern distinct from Shelley's "Spirit of Beauty," that abstract essence of "spirit fair," an "unseen Power" that hovers everywhere within this "dim vast vale of tears."

Ltr. to Fanny
Brawne,
(?) Feb. 1820

A THING of beauty is eternally a source of joy. This is Keats's affirmation in his initial line. Almost at once, he offers a temporal variant of that primal theme: "Its loveliness increases." The theme had been explored earlier with the sonnet, *On the Grasshopper and Cricket*. Then, a similar strain had urged with gentle insistence, "The poetry of earth is never dead"; it is "ceasing never"; it is always "increasing." The following lines of *Endymion* offer yet another variation of that same theme, the recognition that a THING of beauty "will never / Pass into nothingness," that it can never become a no thing. Irreducible, it can only increase its value and its loveliness. It must remain eternally a source of joy. Things beautiful can never become no things, can never pass into a state of nothingness.

Viewed in the light of his March, 1818 letter to Bailey, where Keats had insisted that "every mental pursuit takes its reality and worth from the ardour of the pursuer," much of this opening motif in *Endymion* becomes relatively lucid. Since values are for the main part experiential, no things can be "made Great and dignified by an ardent pursuit." As Keats was to insist in his extended letter to George and Georgiana, "Nothing ever becomes real till it is experienced." Some time before, he had written to Haydon of a similar compulsion, "to form greater things—that is to say, ethereal things— . . . greater things than our Creator himself made." Accordingly, when

Ltr. to George &
Georgiana,
19 Mar. 1819

Ltr. to Haydon,
11 May 1817

Keats speaks in the opening of *Endymion* of a THING of beauty
that "will never / Pass into nothingness," his referent is not the
*spirit* of beauty. Real values reside within the *things* of beauty,
and things real can never become no things. We can increase
their dignity and worth, but we can never diminish from them:
"Therefore, on every morrow, are we wreathing / A flowery
band to bind us to the earth."

Understandably, this symbolic band which ought to bind us
to the world of elemental space is a THING of beauty, not a spirit
—for only through the interaction of mind and heart with the
*things* of earth can true creativity be fulfilled. This is how
poetry is formed, a soul created, a mite added to the mass of
materials harvested from the grand materials surrounding us.

The true creator—of poetry, but also of his own soul—must
bind himself to the earth with the *things* of beauty, we are
reminded in this opening passage of *Endymion*. He must bind
himself, despite "the inhuman dearth of noble natures," despite "despondence" and "all the unhealthy and o'er-darkened
ways / Made for our searching." Pain, despondence, darkness
are no less a part of life, no less a part of the materials that go
into soul-making, than the beautiful and the pleasurable. Divine creation affords the sun, the moon, trees, daffodils, clear
rills, the forest brake, the fair musk-rose; mortal creation can
supply "the grandeur of the dooms . . . imagined," the "lovely
tales . . . heard or read." Therefore, he who would create his
soul must bind himself to mortality with the flowery band.
There should be no regret at man's inability to fly above and
beyond the pains and annoyances, the thorns from which Shelley would be uplifted. Indeed, unless these essences are bound
to us fast, regardless of "whether there be shine, or gloom
o'ercast," we will find ourselves confronted with the inevitability of death, the end of all sensation.

And so, to show that death is the only alternative, unless we
daily wreathe the flowery band that binds us to the earth, Keats
offers to trace the story of Endymion, a mortal who pursues the
ethereal joys inherent in the immortal Cynthia. Because he
leaves behind the world of sensation, abandoning the contents
of the earth for his vision of the spirit of beauty, the shepherd

must ultimately face death. Mind and heart can no longer interact with the grand materials of the world.

Because he comes to recognize the fallacy of his pursuit, Endymion returns before the close of the narrative to the mortal, earthly, sensuous world, where beauty can remain forever a joy, despite the pains and annoyances, the fever and the fret:

> I have clung
> To nothing, lov'd a nothing, nothing seen
> Or felt but a great dream! O I have been
> Presumptuous against love, against the sky,
> Against all elements, against the tie
> Of mortals each to each, against the blooms
> Of flowers, rush of rivers, and the tombs
> Of heroes gone! Against his proper glory
> Has my own soul conspired: so my story
> Will I to children utter, and repent.
> There never liv'd a mortal man, who bent
> His appetite beyond his natural sphere,
> But starv'd and died.

ENDYMION,
*IV, 636–55*

In his pursuit of "a great dream," the world of things has been left behind. He has pursued only "cloudy phantasms" and the "air of visions." But in his renunciation of Cynthia, the ardent shepherd vows that airy voices shall no more cheat him, breathless and aghast, to this "shore of tangled wonder." He has presumed against the things of beauty, the life of sensations, "against love, against the sky, / Against all elements." Now, in reaching for the Indian maid, he turns to one who has redeemed his life "from too thin breathing," aware that only in this mortal love can mortal man create an immortality.

Keats's obsession with the things of beauty—eternally a source of joy and ever increasing—gravitates about a world of forms immediately identifiable as Homeric. Hovering over the palpable, the visible, the sensuous, the nineteenth-century poet would part from the world of things only with the greatest reluctance—much as the author of *The Odyssey* delights in bringing to light all the phenomena of the material world and

in keeping that light shining at its fullest, at its most intense. Neither Keats nor Homer is to be confused with the hedonistic materialism of Edmond and Jules de Goncourt, the economic materialism of Émile Zola, or the mercantilism of Daniel Defoe. With Defoe, the material world is rarely the source of sensation, of internalized feeling. For Moll Flanders and Robinson Crusoe, the world of things is to be identified with security and comfort, status and self-interest. Although Keats may share with the Goncourts an aesthetic delight in the sensuous, missing from Defoe, sensation is not an end in itself for the poet; hedonism for Keats is rarely for the sake of titillation alone, a drive which moved the Goncourts into an eclecticism and a morbid aesthetic, almost pathological. Sensation is for Keats a means of soul-creation. Things are the stuff of poetry, as of life, the lowest rung of the hierarchical ladder ascended by mortal man in the process of forging his identity. Although he shares with Zola the recognition that happiness on earth is dependent upon the manner in which man kneads or is kneaded by these material forces, for Zola method is dependent upon knowledge—a knowledge of the natural laws pervading the universe: economic laws and social, as well as biological. But for Keats, the determining force emanates out of the poet himself, his own intensity, his own ardor, and not from any external law or from an internalized knowledge of these laws.

Endymion's fevered pursuit of the ethereal and the immortal takes him through three distinct phases, not too far removed from those rungs of the hierarchical ladder projected in an earlier exercise which Keats had called *Sleep and Poetry*. There, not unlike Diotima's ladder of ascent in Plato's *Symposium*, aimed at perceiving Absolute Beauty, the poet begins with a series of inquiries, aimed at detecting what is higher in his scale of values than the sensuous things of earth. What is more gentle than a summer wind? more soothing than a pretty bird? "more tranquil than a musk-rose"? "more healthful than the leafiness of dales"? "more secret than a nest of nightingales"? More than all these is sleep. But higher beyond thought than luxurious indolence, "more strange, more beautiful, more smooth, more regal" than either sensuous immersion or indolence is poesy. And higher still than poetry is that state of

"immortality" achieved as the glorious denizen of some wide heaven. How is this heaven to be achieved? First, the poet must

> Write on my tablets all that was permitted,
> All that was for our human senses fitted.
> Then the events of this wide world I'd seize
> Like a strong giant, and my spirit teaze
> Till at its shoulders it should proudly see
> Wings to find out an immortality.

SLEEP AND POETRY, 79–84

Far from outlining a series of discrete steps in a hierarchy of values, the poem suggests some necessary transitions, direct and causal, between sensuous experiences and "immortality." The sensuous interaction of mind and heart with the things of the external world—the wind, nightingales, a musk-rose, a pot of basil—is high on this scale of values. But indolence is higher than this sensuous interaction and a necessary state into which the creator must pass. Indolence or sleep (what Keats was later to identify with "negative capability") transforms the mind into a fit receptacle for every thing and all experiences. Thus, the first interaction, external and sensorial, is a priming experience, the bottom rung of the axiological ladder. To open one's self, through dreams and visions, to an inner penetration of this outer world is a higher experience. But higher still than this inner penetration is the condition of the poet who actively records "all that was for human senses fitted," for he transforms that internalized experience into a new externality: of the old form is created a new identity. Finally, the highest rung is scaled, for having seized upon the physical and external, all that was in this wide world fitted for the senses, the poet can "like a strong giant" tease his spirit—using the sun, the moon, the stars, the earth and its contents, as it were, to form greater things. Thus, he will have grown the wings to seek his immortality. With Cupid's "light pinions," the mortal poet can fan away "All death-shadows, and glooms that overcast" his spirit. From the first chanting notes of the nightingale, ringing out from faery lands forlorn, he can create an ode—an identity—an immortality. Only through an initial ardor of pursuit, with warm

ENDYMION, III, 978–85

pulses, panting bosoms, and dishevelled hair, is true creativity possible.

Even in this brief and early perception, poetry seems to encompass several functions for Keats. It maintains a position within a hierarchy of values. Higher than the pleasurable but discrete senses, it is of lesser value than the "immortality" that attends the creation of the soul. But then, poetry is not only a value in and of itself; it also serves the rather pragmatic function of allowing man to penetrate the secret visions glimpsed but briefly in the world of things—a process somewhat distinct from Wordsworth's transcendence of that world. The poet, as it were, uses the world of sensations in order to create his poetic soul. Thus, it offers to alleviate the pains and bitterness of life, extending a balm "to soothe the cares, and lift the thoughts of man." From a cosmological perspective, it affords a connective link between the realm of mortality and that other realm, what so far is only vaguely described as "immortality." It serves as a gigantic bridge between self and object, the internal being and the externalized thing, the lower reality of the senses and the higher reality of spirit.

SLEEP AND POETRY, 247

This same hierarchical pattern had been suggested earlier in *Sleep and Poetry,* when there appeared a plea

SLEEP AND POETRY, 96–154

> for ten years, that I may overwhelm
> Myself in poesy; so I may do the deed
> That my own soul has to itself decreed.

Initially, the poet writes, "the realm I'll pass / Of Flora, and old Pan." There, he would surrender himself to the sensual pleasures of the pagan world. But these pleasures are not enduring. One must "bid these joys farewell . . . must pass them for a nobler life," to take part in "the agonies, the strife / Of human hearts." Driven in his indolence by the chariot of the imagination, he can indulge in "shapes of delight, of mystery, and fears." But this too is inadequate. He must pass upward yet, must "flit onward" to a mysterious realm which he now has difficulty discerning. And yet, for all the vagueness and mystery, only the supreme power of poesy, "might half slumb'ring on its own right arm," can move him to this higher sphere, fulfilling

SLEEP AND POETRY, 230–47

its "great end": soothing the cares and lifting the thoughts of man.

Although the pattern is as hazy and unformulated in this 1817 poem as in Keats's consoling letter in November of 1817 to Benjamin Bailey, by late January in the following year it had become relatively lucid. The rose-bud had unfolded and revealed the flower. To his publisher John Taylor, Keats wrote of the necessity of revising Endymion's speech to Peona on the *Ltr. to Taylor,* nature of happiness. Taylor, a "consequitive Man," might find *30 Jan. 1818* the revision "as a thing almost of mere words—but I assure you," Keats insisted,

that when I wrote it, it was a regular stepping of the Imagination towards a Truth. My having written that Argument will perhaps be of the greatest Service to me of any thing I ever did—It set before me at once the gradations of Happiness even like a kind of Pleasure Thermometer—and it is my first Step towards the chief Attempt in the Drama—the playing of different Natures with Joy and Sorrow.

The gradations of happiness to which Keats refers, these imaginative steppings toward a Truth, are, as Endymion explains to Peona, the rise from a primary level of "music's kiss . . . old *ENDYMION,* songs . . . old ditties" to the "richer entanglements . . . of love *I, 784–813* and friendship." Only through these steps, it is explained, can man ultimately step

>Into a sort of oneness, and our state
>Is like a floating spirit's. But there are
>Richer entanglements, enthralments far
>More self-destroying, leading, by degrees,
>To the chief intensity: the crown of these
>Is made of love and friendship, and sits high
>Upon the forehead of humanity.
>All its more ponderous and bulky worth
>Is friendship, whence there ever issues forth
>A steady splendour; but at the tip-top,
>There hangs by unseen film, an orbed drop
>Of light, and that is love: its influence,
>Thrown in our eyes, genders a novel sense,
>At which we start and fret; till in the end,

> Melting into its radiance, we blend,
> Mingle, and so become a part of it,—
> Nor with aught else can our souls interknit
> So wingedly . . .

The hazy vision of *Sleep and Poetry* is here, in this reworking of *Endymion*, articulated and fixed. An aesthetic pattern is revealed that was at one with the poet's cosmic and ethical view. Endymion's pursuit of happiness in ethereal, non-mortal beauty takes him with much rambling and an awkward excess through these three pronounced stages which Keats has outlined. At first, the shepherd moves to the festival of Pan. There, through the sensuous god of nature and of song, he strives to materialize his incorporeal vision of Cynthia. The harsh nets of dull mortality, flung over the boundaries of his earth, prevent a flight of the spirit to her endless heaven. And so, when sensation alone proves an insufficiency, Endymion moves into a higher
ENDYMION, realm of love, for "earthly love has power to make / Men's
I, 843–4 being mortal, immortal." Brooding on with ardency, he meets with the great lovers of history—Adonis, Alpheus, Arethusa— and manages to effect a temporary union with the moon-goddess. Now he recognizes the necessity of passion, lifted to a higher state through love:

ENDYMION,
II, 904–9
> Now I have tasted her sweet soul to the core
> All other depths are shallow: essences,
> Once spiritual, are like muddy lees,
> Meant but to fertilize my earthly root,
> And make my branches lift a golden fruit
> Into the bloom . . .

Now, even as his soul stands almost midway from mortality,
ENDYMION, Cynthia promises to win for him "immortal bliss," to snatch
III, 1007–27 him with a kiss into her spiritual air, beyond the fair faint line that separates the sensuous from the ethereal, the physical from the incorporeal, the known from the unknown. This is the point where

                              to him          ENDYMION,
Who lives beyond earth's boundary, grief is dim,          *IV, 619–21*
Sorrow is but a shadow . . .

There is fallen Saturn, parted from heaven, and known not by          HYPERION,
the earth as god. It is the point so clearly delineated in the          *I, 55–6*
sonnet *To Homer,* where

> on the shores of darkness there is light,
> And precipices show untrodden green,
> There is a budding morrow in midnight;
> There is a triple sight in blindness keen . . .

This is the state of immortality toward which Endymion has
been striving, the state of oneness into which we step, through
rich entanglements and enthrallments self-destroying, so that
we blend and mingle, melting into its radiance.

Unlike Diotima's ladder of ascent in *The Symposium,* which
would move men into the absolute and true form of Beauty,
Endymion's hierarchical climb is limited. The light "on the
shores of darkness" comes from behind as well as before. As
with Marlow in Joseph Conrad's heart of darkness, where there
is always the faintest glimmer of light (if only in man's moral
sense which looks into the darkness and can judge: "The horror! the horror!"), there is in Endymion's darkness the faintest
gleam of redemption, the slenderest thread down which the
errant soul can wend a quick descent, back to the world of
"white hawthorn, and the pastoral eglantine." In his embalmed          ODE TO A
darkness, the life of sensation still beckons, if only in the mem-          NIGHTINGALE, *V*
ory of "fast fading violets" and "the fruit-tree wild." Like
Conrad's Marlow who stares into the impenetrable darkness
with only one foot over the abyss, the errant shepherd is permit-
ted to draw back his hesitating foot and return to the world of
merciless logic—the world of light and darkness, of burning
foreheads and of parching tongues.

Conrad's grasp of the real and the ideal is essentially moral;
Keats's, aesthetic. But differences between the novelist and the

poet emerge more from assumptions behind the artistic form
that each adopts. Significance of the Endymion tale for Conrad
would lie, not within, like the kernel of a nut, but outside of it,
dependent upon perspective, the light brought to bear. And,
after all—as Conrad would be the first to assert—the kind of
light brought by Keats upon the adventures of Endymion or
Marlow would differ considerably from that brought by Marlow's aunt or Kurtz's Intended, by Glaucus or the Indian maid.

This relativity of perspective, so crucial to the twentieth century—to Conrad, but also to James and Joyce, to Virginia
Woolf and Faulkner—is singularly foreign to an eighteenth-
century uniformitarian Pope. But for Keats, who faces the
duality of a universe in which self and external nature, the
experiencing *I* and the experienced *it,* are set apart from one
another, the holiness of the self can be enhanced only through
the sensorial absorption of the *it.* The potentialities of man are
to be redeemed only through the ardor of his pursuit, by which
his true self, his true identity can be formed. This is no relativism of perspective that we find in Keats; but then neither is it
an absolutism so implicit in Pope. For Keats, truth lies within
the bounded shell no more than within that halo of surrounding light. It lies rather in the intensity of light man brings to
the kernel; the ardor of experience, as distinct from the colored
and distorted glasses that men wear. It is a matter of experience, not of vision; the degree of color, rather than the kind.

This is precisely what Endymion himself comes to realize,
though belatedly. Through his revival of those lovers who have
been wooed by their ardor to the point of eternal sleep just this
side of death, he comes to recognize that intensity of pursuit
carries with it this terrible paradox: that the greatest intensity
is self-annihilating, for it ultimately denies the world of sensations which is itself the center of its being. Like the scent that
moves to separate itself from the flower, man would move
toward the eternal denial of his own life-giving source. And so,
the shepherd sagely abandons his search before the close, re-
turning to the world of pains and annoyances. In renouncing
his pursuit and allying himself with the mortal Indian maid, he
expresses his recognition that death—the end of sensation, and
therefore the end of soul-making—is the ultimate threat of life

ethereal. One must rather bind one's self to the earth, to the things of the earth, with a band that reeks of mortality. As Keats enjoins in his sonnet to Spenser, "the flower must drink the nature of the soil" before it can blossom. Endymion, in his presumption "against the tie of mortals each to each," has loved a very nothing.

These two passages in *Endymion*—the opening exposition on the eternality of joy in a THING of beauty, and the speech to Peona on the hierarchical rungs that lead to happiness—provide the theme and structure of the larger narrative. But also, and with infinite variation, they offer the basic motif and development of Keats's other poetry, the hierarchy of values confronting any creator who must forge his identity from the "three grand materials acting the one upon the other for a series of years."

For Shelley, like Plato, the painful, the dark, the mortal, the ignoble, the unhealthy, only indicate the remoteness of the soul from divine form. Life's dome of multicolored glass stains the white radiance of eternity. Bent and chained to earthly shadows, like the men in Plato's parable, Shelley would fly with his skylark from the changing, passing Many. But with Keats, the One can be seen only through the Many; the white radiance of eternity is discernible only through the glass of multi-colors. Eternity is visible only within the human condition. Falling upon the thorns of life and bleeding, far from being undesirable, is an essential concomitant of that condition, the bitterness that must attend the sweet, the pain so interwoven with the pleasure, where even nothings can be made great and dignified through the ardor of our pursuit.

"This is the world," Keats writes to George and Georgiana. ". . . Circumstances are like Clouds continually gathering and bursting—While we are laughing the seed of some trouble is put into the wide arable land of events—while we are laughing it sprouts . . . grows and suddenly bears a poison fruit which we must pluck."

*Ltr. to George & Georgiana, 19 Mar. 1819*

"This is human life," Keats reiterates in *Endymion:*

ENDYMION, *II, 153–8*

the war, the deeds,
The disappointment, the anxiety,

>Imagination's struggles, far and nigh,
>All human; bearing in themselves this good,
>That they are still the air, the subtle food,
>To make us feel existence . . .

All-absorbing, all-encompassing, the new divinity rejects nothing from the materials that may potentially become his air and food. They bear within themselves this good, "to make us feel existence." Here is Keats's counter to the creed expounded by the Age of "Reason," the Cartesian *cogito ergo sum—I think, therefore I am*. Keatsian existence must be predicated upon feeling, instead of thinking. The classicism of the rationalists has been modified by a new resolve: *sentio ergo sum—I feel, therefore I am*.

*Endymion Sleeping*
a Greek relief (first century B.C.)
Capitoline Museum, Rome

Sarcophagus with the story
of Diana and Endymion
(first half of the second century A.D.)
Capitoline Museum, Rome

*Endymion and the
Moon*, G. B. Cima
(c. 1459–1517)
National Gallery,
Parma

*Endymion Sleeping*
Anne-Louis Girodet (1767–1824)
The Louvre, Paris

*Selene and Endymion*
Nicolas Poussin (1594–1665)
Detroit Institute of Arts

*Endymion and Selene*
Michel François André-Bardon (1700–1785)
California Palace of the Legion of Honor

*Diana and Endymion*
Peter Paul Rubens (1577–1640)
National Gallery, London

*Diana Visiting Endymion*
Wedgwood plaque (c. 1785)
Wedgwood Museum, England

*The Elgin Marbles*
East Frieze
Left, four heroes conversing
Right, seated, Hermes, Dionysos,
Demeter, and Ares
The British Museum, London

"What leaf-fring'd legend haunts about thy shape
Of deities or mortals, or of both,
In Tempe or the dales of Arcady?"

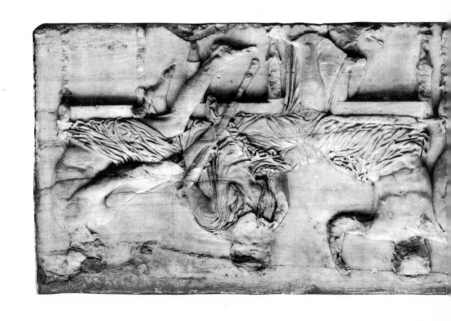

*The Elgin Marbles*
South Frieze
The British Museum, London

"To what green altar, O mysterious priest,
Lead'st thou that heifer lowing at the skies,
And all her silken flanks with garlands drest?"

# 7

# An Operational Mode:
# The Sympathetic Imagination

In his lengthy discourse on the "vale of Soul-making" Keats had written of three grand materials and the interaction necessary to form the intelligence or soul "destined to possess the sense of Identity." And to Peona, before delineating the hierarchical ladder leading to happiness, Endymion had spoken of a "sort of oneness" toward which our minds are beckoned, "a fellowship with essence" into which we can mingle and blend, the ultimate identity we are destined to possess.

*Ltr. to George & Georgiana, 15 Apr. 1819*

ENDYMION, *I, 777–811*

An examination of the *objects* or *materials* of Keats's aesthetic process is, of course, only the initial step in comprehending the creative process. The second, of necessity, must concern itself with the *operational mode* through which the imagination can step toward a "chief intensity" into a "oneness," the precise *means* by which "fellowship with essence" can be created. By what means can the human heart gain an identity? How can man form a soul? What is the way in which "the Earth and its Contents" can be transformed by the creative artist into "greater things than our Creator himself made"? Through what procedure can nothing be so ardently pursued as to be made great and dignified, possessing reality and worth?

Perhaps the most illuminating account of this operational

mode is contained in a late 1818 letter in which Keats endeav
ors to explain to Richard Woodhouse the nature of creative
genius. Woodhouse, a legal adviser to Keats's publishers, had
been greatly impressed with the poet's creative powers. During
the life of Keats and afterwards, he devoted himself to collect-
ing and recording a wealth of materials from and about the
poet:

*Ltr. to Woodhouse,*
*27 Oct. 1818*

As to the poetical Character itself, (I mean that sort of which, if I am any
thing, I am a Member; that sort distinguished from the wordsworthian or
egotistical sublime; which is a thing per se and stands alone) it is not itself
—it has no self—it is every thing and nothing—It has no character—it
enjoys light and shade; it lives in gusto, be it foul or fair, high or low, rich
or poor, mean or elevated—It has as much delight in conceiving an Iago as
an Imogen. What shocks the virtuous philosopher, delights the camelion
Poet. It does no harm from its relish of the dark side of things any more
than from its taste for the bright one; because they both end in speculation. A Poet is the most unpoetical of any thing in existence; because he
has no Identity—he is continually in for—and filling some other Body—
The Sun, the Moon, the Sea and Men and Women who are creatures of
impulse are poetical and have about them an unchangeable attribute—the
poet has none; no identity—he is certainly the most unpoetical of all God's
creatures. If then he has no self, and if I am a Poet, where is the Wonder
that I should say I would write no more? . . . not one word I ever utter
can be taken for granted as an opinion growing out of my identical nature
—how can it, when I have no nature? When I am in a room with People if
I ever am free from speculating on creations of my own brain, then not
myself goes home to myself: but the identity of every one in the room
begins so to press upon me that, I am in a very little time annihilated—not
only among Men; it would be the same in a Nursery of children. . . . But
even now I am perhaps not speaking from myself; but from some character
in whose soul I now live.

Initially, in this examination of the nature of genius, the
"wordsworthian or egotistical sublime" is distinguished from
"the poetical Character [which] . . . has no self . . . no character . . . no Identity." For the "egotistical sublime," uniqueness
of self remains paramount, while the true poetical character is
easily affected by everything. It relishes light and shade, fair
and foul, high and low. With equal intensity and unrestrained
gusto, it welcomes the bitter and the sweet. Nothing is excluded
from the province of the poet. He can assume the character of
an Iago, as well as an Imogen. Having no identity himself, he

can all the more easily project his self into the sea, the moon, the sun, as well as men and women, always "filling some other Body." Somehow, he manages to dissolve those isolating barriers which the "egotistical sublime" seems intent upon preserving, the barriers between the human heart and the things of elemental space—things real, things semi-real, and no things.

This annihilating process, aimed at dissolving the isolating boundaries between self and the external world, is typical of the nineteenth-century romantic. There is Walt Whitman who would embrace all and reject nothing; but there is also the single-minded Heathcliff of Emily Brontë's *Wuthering Heights* who strikes loose the sides of Catherine's coffin the night of her burial, and dreams "of dissolving with her, and being more happy still."

The poetic mode in Keats is characterized by this dissolving process. Lycius strives toward this end with Lamia the serpent woman:

> How to entangle, trammel up and snare
> Your soul in mine, and labyrinth you there
> Like the hid scent in an unbudded rose?

LAMIA, *II, 52–4*

In the sonnet to Reynolds, Keats longs for the same ideal, that a week might stretch into an age, a single year into a thousand, so that the warm flush of meeting and of parting might be eternally prolonged:

> So could we live long life in little space,
> So time itself would be annihilate . . .

TO J. R.

In his sonnet on Dante, the lyricist has apparently been "so charm'd, so conquer'd" in his reading of the Paolo and Francesca episode that he is himself enabled to descend to that "second circle of sad hell":

ON A DREAM

> —pale were the sweet lips I saw,
> Pale were the lips I kiss'd, and fair the form
> I floated with, about that melancholy storm.

By far the clearest exposition of this annihilating process occurs in the *Ode to a Nightingale*. Here, the nightingale is not to be defined within pre-determined categories—as an ornithological species; as a genus about which lyrical poetry is traditionally written; or even as a bird befitting the classical ode form. Reality of bird and self is wholly contingent upon what is done with the bird by the singer, and what the bird does to that mortal songster. Interaction establishes both their identities. Projection of the sympathetic imagination is not only independent of pre-established categories, but it aims at breaking down these categories whenever they are to be found. Thus, Keats's nightingale, dissociated from any classical context, is identified at once with the delights of immediate song. The "immortal Bird" in its melodious plot sings in its happiness of eternal summer, a curious contrast with the mortal poet whose heart does ache. It resembles less the Philomel of Ovid than the "double-lived" bird in *Bards of Passion and of Mirth*, a happy songster who communes with spheres of moon and sun, as well as with the passion and the spite of mortals:

> . . . the nightingale doth sing
> Not a senseless, tranced thing,
> But divine melodious truth;
> Philosophic numbers smooth;
> Tales and golden histories
> Of heaven and its mysteries.

Obsessed with a disparity between his own drugged senses and the "full-throated' ease" of this light-winged Dryad, the poet longs for the dissolution of his "drowsy numbness." He would join the immortal bird in some dim forest.

At first, dissolution of spatial barriers separating poet from bird, numbness from ease, seems possible from sensation alone, through the use of intoxicants—Bacchus "with beaded bubbles winking at the brim." But before long, this inferior mode of pursuit is dismissed. Instead, the poet is determined to be charioted only by his own creativity, through the "viewless wings of Poesy."

Away! away! for I will fly to thee,
   Not charioted by Bacchus and his pards,
But on the viewless wings of Poesy,
   Though the dull brain perplexes and retards:
Already with thee! tender is the night,
   And haply the Queen-Moon is on her throne,
     Cluster'd around by all her starry Fays;
      But here there is no light,
   Save what from heaven is with the breezes blown
     Through verdurous glooms and winding mossy ways.

ODE TO A
NIGHTINGALE, *IV–VI*

Almost at once, the pursuer leaps forward to merge with the pursued. Not space alone, but time is annihilated. Out of this passing night of "leaden-eyed despairs," he somehow leaps into a changeless world. "Though the dull brain perplexes," a mystical merging of the two singers seems almost complete, as he begins to call jubilantly to the invisible songster, "Already with thee!" .

And yet, not wholly. Aware that he has "been half in love with easeful Death," the poet stands poised upon a midnight point:

I cannot see what flowers are at my feet,
   Nor what soft incense hangs upon the boughs,
But, in embalmed darkness, guess each sweet
   Wherewith the seasonable month endows
The grass, the thicket, and the fruit-tree wild;
   White hawthorn, and the pastoral eglantine;
     Fast fading violets cover'd up in leaves;
      And mid-May's eldest child,
   The coming musk-rose, full of dewy wine,
     The murmurous haunt of flies on summer eves. ·

Ahead is "embalmed darkness" and no-time; behind are the seasonable months of calendrical time, endowing grass and thicket with every sweet. Too ardent a pursuit brings complete self-annihilation and death, the end of human time and of all sensation.

Darkling I listen; and, for many a time
  I have been half in love with easeful Death,
Call'd him soft names in many a mused rhyme,
  To take into the air my quiet breath;
Now more than ever seems it rich to die,
  To cease upon the midnight with no pain,
    While thou art pouring forth thy soul abroad
      In such an ecstasy!
  Still wouldst thou sing, and I have ears in vain—
    To thy high requiem become a sod.

Rather than "become a sod" to song, the mortal lyricist is tolled
back to "sole self" from his near-union with the bird. Tolled
back from his ethereal pursuit of the invisible bird, he can
write an ode—he can wreathe once more the flowery band that
shall bind him to the earth. Like Endymion, his life has been
ENDYMION,   redeemed "from too thin breathing," from airy voices that have
IV, 650–5   lulled him "to the shore / Of tangled wonder, breathless and
aghast."

The experience undergone by the singer in *Ode to a Nightingale* is not wholly incomprehensible to the modern reader,
although the temptation has been to examine the imaginative
leap in terms more mystical than Freudian, more consonant
with the "dark night of the soul" than with infantile repressions, demands of the libido, or creation of a pleasure ego. Yet
the ode reveals with painful clarity a search, recognizable to the
twentieth-century mind, for palliatives through the use of intoxicants. The sonnet to Reynolds can be labeled "wishful
thinking." The sonnet on Dante, identified as a dream, is somewhat revealing of "repressed wishes." In the passage from
*Lamia,* sex as a powerful diversion can allow Lycius to care
little for worldly pain.

Seemingly, Keats is moving in all these poems toward the
pleasure principle about which Freud is so apprehensive. Yet
for Keats, love is synonymous with fellow-feeling, sympathy,
brotherhood. It is moral and social, as well as aesthetic. Ardent and intensive, love alone can obliterate the spatial and
temporal boundaries between ego and object, between the internal which is always sharply delineated and the enticing blur

of externality. Lycius would obliterate the corporeal boundaries between himself and Lamia; Keats would dissolve the spatio-temporal bounds that separate him from Reynolds; the hazy line dividing legend from life, lovers in *The Inferno* from lovers of love, must be demolished in the sonnet on Dante; and in the nightingale ode, physical differences that distinguish his own anguished song from the full-throated ease of the bird must somehow be dissipated. But the external world is never really threatening for Keats; it always bears within it the power to make us feel existence, the means by which we can create our identity. There is never in Keats the attempt to dissociate from his own ego all that gives rise to pain. He knows too well that suffering can be traced from his own heart and thoughts, his own mortal condition, his own relationship with other men and with the things of the external world. Perhaps the closest Keats approaches the creation of a pleasure ego is in his relationship with Fanny Brawne, where love is selfish rather than sympathetic, turned inward rather than outward. In a letter to Fanny, he expresses both delight and trepidation that his passion is rapidly becoming his self-interest:

ENDYMION, II, 156–8

My love has made me selfish. . . . You have absorb'd me. I have a sensation at the present moment as though I was dissolving. . . . I have been astonished that Men could die Martyrs for religion—I have shudder'd at it —I shudder no more—I could be martyr'd for my Religion—Love is my religion—I could die for that—I could die for you. My Creed is Love and you are its only tenet—You have ravish'd me away by a Power I cannot resist. . . . My love is selfish.

*Ltr. to Fanny Brawne, 13 Oct. 1819*

For Keats, the imaginative experience, sympathetically turned outward, is explicable no more in Freudian terms than in those apparent in the mystic vision of St. John of the Cross. For Keats, as for the early nineteenth century in general—and in particular, for William Hazlitt from whom the poet seems to have imbibed liberally—the experience is more closely analogous to the social and ethical tenets of the sympathetic imagination described by Adam Smith in his *Theory of Moral Sentiments.*

Almost a half century before, Smith had outlined a position equally removed from the rationalists, who were insistent that

morality was derived from reason alone, and from the empiricists, who were maintaining that ethical powers could be attributed to the senses. Smith insisted upon the presence in man of
an imaginative faculty, almost a sixth sense, medial to both the
passions and the understanding:

Though our brother is upon the rack, as long as we ourselves are at our
ease, our senses will never inform us of what he suffers. They never did,
and never can carry us beyond our own person, and it is by the imagination only that we can form any conception of what are his sensations. . . .
It is the impression of our senses only, not those of his, which our
imaginations copy. By the imagination we place ourselves in his
situation. . . .

The sympathetic imagination carries man beyond his person to
"inform" him of his brother's suffering upon the rack. For
Smith, the imagination functions with powers relegated by the
empiricists to the senses, though also with some of the judging
powers attributed by the rationalists to the understanding.

Smith's conception of the sympathetic imagination is developed at length in the early writings of William Hazlitt. But in
most of Hazlitt's later essays, sympathy is extended to form a
link between the moral and the aesthetic through "gusto," the
intensity of ardor by which the individual can turn emotions
outwardly. Self is drawn into the external world through the
sympathetic imagination, but self can fuse with surrounding
objects through gusto, by defining the objects through power
and passion. Thus, in *Genius and Common Sense* Wordsworth
emerges as "the greatest egotist," one who "sits in the centre of
his own being," because he has a "mind averse from outward
objects, but ever intent upon its own workings." The reverse of
the chameleon who borrows color from all about him, Wordsworth sheds his own coloring on all that lies outside of self. He
is an ordinary genius, "exclusive and self-willed," finding little
of permanent interest beyond the self—and quite the contrary
of the real genius of Shakespeare who could take on the character of what was outside of him, because he possessed "the
faculty of transforming himself at will into whatever he chose."
Hazlitt's terminology, and his appraisal of Shakespeare and
Wordsworth, are almost identical with that revealed in Keats's
letter to Woodhouse about the "poetical Character." Yet the

terms are also most apparent in Coleridge's comparison of Milton's "intense egotism" and Shakespeare: "Shakespere's poetry is characterless; that is, it does not reflect the individual Shakespere; but John Milton himself is in every line of the 'Paradise Lost.'" Generally, Smith's theory, without Hazlitt's emendation, is most pervasive in the romantics, particularly Wordsworth and Shelley. Without Hazlitt's idea of gusto, however, the sympathetic imagination provides only a moral and social basis for art. With Keats, the implications of gusto are further extended to form an aesthetic, as well as a cosmology, wholly dependent upon the ardor of pursuit.

For Keats, as for Hazlitt, sensation provides the essential spark for moral and social illumination. Unless the spark lights the torch of the imagination, men are doomed to grope their way in darkness and isolation. The burnings of the human heart are not to be denied. The heart itself "must first feel and suffer in a thousand diverse ways." It must suffer with the foul, even while delighting in the fair. But unless it kindles the imagination, sensation must turn inwards, burning itself into the socket. Alone, the affections are like a pilotless ship; but Invention is "the Polar Star of Poetry, as Fancy is the Sails, and Imagination the Rudder." Without the directing social and moral powers of the sympathetic imagination, feelings must remain self-contained, incapable of penetrating other hearts and minds. Isolated from other sparks of creation, the heart maintains its own limited integrity, its self-love, its egocentric cravings. It is a "thing per se and stands alone," like the ascetic beadsman in *The Eve of St. Agnes,* who aspires to spiritual existence even while avoiding the life of sensations because these are condemned (falsely) by religion. Impervious to "Love's fev'rous citadel," where he is surrounded by burning Porphyro and panting Madeline, he prefers to walk along the chapel aisle with fingers numb and frosted breath, beside the frozen, sculptured dead. Before the close of the narrative the burning Porphyro can melt through love into the dreams of Madeline, as the rose blends its odor with the violet; but the beadsman can anticipate only a frosted, lonely grave. After a thousand *aves,* unseeking and "unsought for [he] slept among his ashes cold."

*Ltr. to Bailey, 8 Oct. 1817*

This same disdain of asceticism is apparent in Keats's sonnet, *Written in Disgust of Vulgar Superstition*. By denying the life of sensations, false religion turns man inward upon himself, promoting rather cares and gloom than fireside joys and Lydian airs.

> The church bells toll a melancholy round,
>     Calling the people to some other prayers,
>     Some other gloominess, more dreadful cares,
> More hearkening to the sermon's horrid sound.
> Surely the mind of man is closely bound
>     In some black spell; seeing that each one tears
>     Himself from fireside joys, and Lydian airs,
> And converse high of those with glory crown'd.
> Still, still they toll, and I should feel a damp—
>     A chill as from a tomb, did I not know
> That they are dying like an outburnt lamp;
>     That 'tis their sighing, wailing ere they go
>     Into oblivion;—that fresh flowers will grow,
> And many glories of immortal stamp.

ISABELLA,
*XVII–XVIII*

In *Isabella* the heroine's two brothers are similarly doomed to a soulless existence. "Self-retired / In hungry pride and gainful cowardice," they worship only at the sterile altar of money. They are incapable of projecting their imagination into others. Only gold and silver are the concern of these "ledger-men" with "vision covetous and sly." Lacking the imagination that will carry them beyond their own person, "these money-bags" cannot conceive a love except for self. They have no love of others, just as they can scarcely comprehend the love that others have —the love of Isabella for Lorenzo or for the pot of basil that flourishes upon his severed head:

ISABELLA, *LVIII*

>             . . . Her brethren wonder'd much
>     Why she sat drooping by the basil green,
> And why it flourish'd, as by magic touch;
>     Greatly they wonder'd what the thing might mean:
> They could not surely give belief, that such
>     A very nothing would have power to wean

> Her from her own fair youth, and pleasures gay,
> And even remembrance of her love's delay.

Using the same techniques developed with the Endymion myth, Keats reinterprets Boccaccio's tale of Isabella and invests it with new meaning, in accord with his own value system. The mercantilism of the brothers, simply an occupational detail in *The Decameron,* is transformed by Keats into an evil, the self-love which counters the promptings of the sympathetic imagination. In Boccaccio the brothers murder Lorenzo to redeem the honor of the family; but Keats stresses their egotism and lack of love.

Religion and money both promote our egocentric cravings, the "egotistical sublime" contrasted by Keats with "the poetical Character itself." The chameleon poet has no identity, for he is forever being formed, being continually in some other body. He is not himself. He has no self, no character, for he is at once nothing and everything. Having once been created, he must perpetually recreate himself and add a mite to his own grand materials. He cannot come home to himself after being in a room with people, for through the sympathetic imagination, self is very soon annihilated in proportion to the identity of everyone in the room beginning to press upon him. "Men who live together have a silent moulding and influencing power over each other," Keats was to write to George and Georgiana. "They interassimulate." A year later, he wrote again to Georgiana: "The worst of Men are those whose self interests are their passion—the next those whose passions are their self-interest."

With Keats, the sympathetic imagination is hardly restricted, of course, to a mimesis of our sensual impressions of men and women, on or off the rack. It can converge upon a nightingale, a Grecian urn, Burns's cottage, grasshoppers and crickets, the autumnal season. ". . . If a sparrow come before my Window," he writes, "I take part in its existence and pick about the Gravel." Of a beautiful woman met in one brief encounter, he finds, "I forget myself entirely because I live in her." Woodhouse recalls in his *Scrapbook* that Keats could "conceive of a billiard Ball that it may have a sense of delight from its own roundness, smoothness . . . . volubility & the rapidity of its mo-

*Ltr. to George & Georgiana, 21 Sept. 1819*

*Ltr. to Georgiana, 15 Jan. 1820*

*Ltr. to Bailey, 22 Nov. 1817*

*Ltr. to George & Georgiana, 14 Oct. 1818*

tion," and he insists in a letter to Tom Taylor that the poet was
"able to throw his own soul into . . . any object he sees or
imagines, so as to see feel . . . be sensible of, & express, all that
the object itself would see feel . . . be sensible of or express."
Keats himself was to explain with seeming relish, "The Sward
is richer for the tread of a real, nervous, english foot—the
eagles nest is finer for the Mountaineer has look'd into it,"
the worth of each having increased through the intensity of the
imaginative pursuit. Not only is a "mite" added to the worth of
self, then, but the value of both sward and nest is enhanced,
each having been made more great and dignified by "an ardent
pursuit—which by and by stamps the burgundy mark on the
bottles of our Minds, insomuch as they are able to *'consecrate
whate'er they look upon.'*" With a kiss of the spirit, things
semi-real are made real. With a lasting embrace of the ardent
pursuer, no things are given worth. Meanwhile, we too assume
greater reality and worth. The mountaineer is finer for having
looked into the eagle's nest; the foot is richer for its tread upon
the sward. The heart that darts into the sparrow which picks
about the gravel is on the way toward forming a soul.

*Ltr. to Bailey,
13 Mar. 1818*

Because values for Keats are experiential, reality and worth
can be achieved only through the intensity of mortal pursuit.
Our minds *"consecrate whate'er they look upon,"* adding their
mite to the things of elemental space. The true priest of Psyche
builds a fane "in some untrodden region of [his] mind." But
the false priest, like Shelley in his *Hymn to Intellectual Beauty,*
will dedicate his powers to a "SPIRIT fair," a visitor "from some
sublimer world" outside the realm of human time, a

ODE TO PSYCHE, *51*

> Spirit of Beauty, that dost consecrate
>   With thine own hues all thou dost shine upon
>   Of human thought or form . . .

For Shelley the world of things reflects reality only insofor as it
is consecrated by a spark of beauty's divine power. Disdaining
this "vale of tears," Shelley would seek above and beyond this
mortal vale for reality and worth. But within his "vale of
Soul-making," Keats is insistent upon man's own creative and
consecrating powers. For Psyche, the "latest born and loveliest

vision far / Of all Olympus' faded hierarchy," and therefore ODE TO PSYCHE, 24–49 without temple, altar, virgin-choir, without shrine or grove or incense sweet, he would with his own branched thoughts

> . . . be thy choir, and make a moan
> Upon the midnight hours;
> Thy voice, thy lute, thy pipe, thy incense sweet
> From swinged censer teeming;
> Thy shrine, thy grove, thy oracle, thy heat
> Of pale-mouth'd prophet dreaming.

In its creation of an identity, Keats's sympathetic imagination can annihilate the boundaries that separate the hours of clock-time and the weeks and days of calendrical-time. Reality and worth for Keats are both possible and necessary only within human time-dimensions. Unlike Shelley, Keats's "second deity" need not move outside of human time to discover his own identity. Poised between embalmed darkness, the no-time of the nightingale and the seasonable months of mortal existence, the singer in Keats's ode must be tolled back to "sole self." Hovering about the Grecian urn, that "foster-child of silence and slow time," the poet retains a truth which is all he needs to know on earth. Breaking down the externalized bounds dividing space and time into discrete chronometric units, the new deity must create an existence within a perpetuity of human time. An eternal *durée* is the only time dimension of the imagination. Because Shelley's spirit of beauty exists *outside* of human time, its ethereal nature partakes of the timeless; while mortal man, confined within the bounds of clock-time, is blessed only with an occasional touch of the ethereal wings of this mystery. Thus, nothing can remain about the colossal wreck of Ozymandias but decay and barren sands, the passing world of mutability. However, for Keats, essence as well as existence, value as well as reality, are available *within* the perpetuity of human time. False religion may define our Being outside the mortal condition. Egotism may confine its own existence to the passing moment. But the true creative poet, intent on merging the moment with all-time, the present with the perpetual, self with others, develops his own essence with-

out the externalized and deceptive antitheses of life and death, mortality and immortality, clock-time and no-time.

Thus, as an essential counterpart to its role in destroying the ego, the sympathetic imagination has the capacity to annihilate external dimensions of space and time. With the strengthening of the imagination, any desire can blossom into a reality:

TO J. R.

> O that a week could be an age, and we
>     Felt parting and warm meeting every week,
> Then one poor year a thousand years would be,
>     The flush of welcome ever on the cheek:
> So could we live long life in little space,
>     So time itself would be annihilate,
> So a day's journey in oblivious haze
>     To serve our joys would lengthen and dilate.
> O to arrive each Monday morn from Ind!
>     To land each Tuesday from the rich Levant!
> In little time a host of joys to bind,
>     And keep our souls in one eternal pant!
> This morn, my friend, and yester evening taught
> Me how to harbour such a happy thought.

As his imagination strengthens, Keats begins to feel more and more every day that he lives not "in this world alone but in a thousand worlds":

*Ltr. to George & Georgiana, 24 Oct. 1818*

No sooner am I alone than shapes of epic greatness are stationed around me, and serve my Spirit. . . . According to my state of mind I am with Achilles shouting in the Trenches or with Theocritus in the Vales of Sicily. Or I throw my whole being into Troilus, and repeating those lines, 'I wander, like a lost soul upon the stygian Banks staying for waftage,' I melt into the air with a voluptuousness so delicate that I am content to be alone. . . . I have written this that you might see I have my share of the highest pleasures and that though I may choose to pass my days alone I shall be no Solitary.

*Ltr. to George & Georgiana, 31 Dec. 1818*

His brother George is assured that "his enjoyment in the different states of human society must depend upon the Powers of his [own] Mind." Visions of an Olympic game or a Roman triumph are no less possible for his brother than for Keats

himself, though their external eye may have paraded before it only the manners and fashions of one country during one age. The inner eye of the sympathetic imagination can remedy that shortcoming, for "manners and customs long since passed whether among the Babylonians or the Bactrians are as real, or even more real than those among which I now live."

Ancient customs "are as real, or even more real," only because the imagination of the creative artist lives in an eternity of time and an infinity of space, as do his creations. Through sympathy, the music of the nightingale can in a moment span the temporal gap between this passing night and all those ancient days when it was heard by emperor and clown:

> Perhaps the self-same song that found a path
>   Through the sad heart of Ruth, when, sick for home,
>     She stood in tears amid the alien corn;
>       The same that oft-times hath
>   Charm'd magic casements, opening on the foam
>   Of perilous seas, in faery lands forlorn.

ODE TO A NIGHTINGALE, *VII*

To the imaginative spirit, a thing of beauty can become a joy forever; for the sympathetic mortal, the cricket's song provides a warmth eternally increasing. The spirit of the great poet never slumbers; it rolls forever about human ears. A moment of supreme ecstasy can accompany Keats's vision of a lock of Milton's hair, thinking he "had beheld it from the flood." Surely, the frieze on the Grecian urn that does remain "when old age shall this generation waste" survives within this same eternality. The youth beneath the trees, captured by the imagination of the creative artist, can never leave his song; the boughs can never shed their leaves; forever will the melodist pipe songs forever new. Only through the imagination can love be "for ever warm and still to be enjoy'd / For ever panting, and for ever young."

LINES ON SEEING A LOCK OF MILTON'S HAIR

# 8

# An Operational Mode:
# The Dreams of Easy Indolence

Even in his earliest verse, Keats had been exploring the role of easy indolence in invoking the powers of imagination. Sleep, dreams, indolence, silence, quiet, awakening—these chords resound with frequency throughout the labyrinth of the poet. Sometimes, as in *Sleep and Poetry,* the larger imaginative experience may be encompassed by an opening and closing apostrophe to tranquillity. This is a state from which the creative act seems to arise and toward which it ultimately descends again. Occasionally, the poem as a whole may offer an encomium, as in the sonnet *To Sleep* and the *Ode on Indolence.* Perhaps the poem itself is marked as a dream, like the *Fall of Hyperion* or the sonnet on Dante. Often a burst of lyricism may lead the reader into soft silence and a shaded bower—as with the *Bright Star* sonnet, *When I Have Fears, On the Grasshopper and Cricket, On First Looking into Chapman's Homer,* or *To One Who Has Been Long in City Pent.* But with frequency the subtle merging of dreaming and the waking state may interpenetrate the entirety of the verse: with *Endymion, La Belle Dame, Isabella, The Eve of St. Agnes.* In the *Ode to Psyche* the poet asks himself with no small confusion, "Surely I dreamt to-day, or did I see / The winged Psyche with awaken'd

eyes?" In *Hyperion* the golden-bowed Apollo declares with the same bewilderment, "I have beheld these eyes before . . . Or I have dream'd." In the *Ode to a Nightingale* the lyricist is confronted with similar befuddlement: "Was it a vision, or a waking dream? . . . Do I wake or sleep?"

A similar interpenetration of dreams and the waking state permeates most of the Shakespearean comedies. In *The Comedy of Errors,* Antipholus of Syracusa begins to wonder if he can trust his senses:

> Am I in earth, in Heaven, or in Hell?
> Sleeping or waking?

In *A Midsummer Night's Dream,* Demetrius articulates the same concern:

> Are you sure
> That we are awake? It seems to me
> That yet we sleep, we dream  . . .

In *Much Ado About Nothing,* Leonato begins to doubt his sight and his hearing: "Are these things spoken, or do I but dream?"

The problem is not limited to the disguises, the magic potions, the confused identities that pervade the comedies. With greater subtlety, Shakespeare invokes a deep distrust throughout the tragedies of what we apprehend during our waking state by means of eye and ear. Lear and Othello come to learn eventually what Bassanio in *The Merchant of Venice* understands quite early, about the deceptiveness of outer show and ornament, of external forms and appearances. Sleep may indeed knit "up the raveled sleave of care" and provide the "balm of hurt minds," as Lady Macbeth realizes, but only by lulling the sleeper from the harsh world of deception into a world of pleasant fantasy and airy shapes. The dreamer and the poet both move into a reality that bears its own truth and that bears constant reminder, during the waking and non-poetic state, of the deceptive world of appearances. In *A Midsummer Night's Dream,* Theseus discourses on this role of the poet:

Lovers and madmen have such seething brains,
Such shaping fantasies, that apprehend
More than cool reason ever comprehends.
The lunatic, the lover, and the poet
Are of imagination all compact.
One sees more devils than vast Hell can hold,
That is the madman. The lover, all as frantic,
Sees Helen's beauty in a brow of Egypt.
The poet's eye, in a fine frenzy rolling,
Doth glance from heaven to earth, from earth to heaven,
And as imagination bodies forth
The forms of things unknown, the poet's pen
Turns them to shapes, and gives to airy nothing
A local habitation and a name.

From the world of dreams, as from the poet's pen, a new reality can emerge for Shakespeare. The distinctive categories of heaven and hell, good and evil, appearances and reality, man and woman, outer and inner, the face and the mask—all are deliberately broken down, "as imagination bodies forth / The forms of things unknown." In Shakespeare, the problem is essentially ontological; but in Keats, where the imagination is primarily sympathetic, the interpenetration of dreams and the waking state is basically aesthetic and ethical. The dreams of mortals who have surrendered before the dull opiate of sleep and indolence are for Keats the greatest inducement to the operations of the sympathetic imagination, just as egotism, youth, and death are the greatest deterrents.

Keats's concern in this visionary state—like Kafka's and Proust's—is with the drama of the inner consciousness. It is a drama distinct from that of Defoe or Zola, almost wholly externalized and concentrating upon things and events. Yet even in his dream-like state, the nineteenth-century poet reveals no Kafka-esque condition. Conflicts taking place within the Keatsian state are not intended to reveal the hidden workings of the unconscious, where reality and worth are wholly dependent upon the troubled dreams of a Joseph K. or Gregor Samsa. Interaction between subject and object, between self and the external world, is in Keats a necessary preliminary to essence.

Interaction that begins in the world of sensations moves with rapidity into the Keatsian world of visions, the imaginative state induced by dreams and by indolence. Keats may share with Kafka the need to create a new and personal mythology; but Keats's myths are meaningful because they represent the poet's own interaction with given materials. In Kafka, we are offered rather the private mythology of men who can no longer interact, for whom the privacy of the internalized dream is all the world that remains—solitary, elusive, nightmarish, and with neither present nor future. Joseph K. dies like a dog; Gregor Samsa, like a gigantic cockroach. And neither one knows how to live or how to die more like a man and less like an animal. Like most of Faulkner's characters, each is caught within the intricacy of his own private world, a world in which the possibilities of the present have been destroyed by the inevitability of the past. This is a world not too far removed from the deterministic things and forces in Zola's universe, where man must always be a victim, and never a hero; a cockroach, and never a human. One is forever doomed to be evasive of his own being, his own mortality.

But in *Sleep and Poetry,* the world of dreams appears as an essential rung on a hierarchical ladder ascended by the spirit in search of its identity. Passive, serene, soothing, full of visions, the dream-like state lends itself best to the operations of the creative imagination. Because the imagination is not yet strong enough to sustain the fullness of the vision at this early date, the dream is sharply broken midway in the poem and displaced by "a sense of real things." Shapes of mystery and delight have vanished:

> The visions are all fled . . .
> Into the light of heaven, and in their stead
> A sense of real things comes doubly strong,
> And, like a muddy stream, would bear along
> My soul to nothingness . . .

SLEEP AND POETRY, *155-9*

Whatever may be worthy in these rhymes, Keats confesses, he partly owes to "sleep, quiet with his poppy coronet."

SLEEP AND POETRY, *348-9*

In *Endymion,* the imagination is equally dependent upon

the strength of the dream for its operational role. Here a year of poetic maturation and the quasi-dramatic form, contrasting with the quasi-didactic form of *Sleep and Poetry,* can sustain the vision over some of the four thousand lines, as the protagonist goes in pursuit of that which becks his ready mind "to fellowship divine." The intensity of his dream-like vision of immortal Cynthia evades all words and rational thought:

ENDYMION,
*I, 572–8*

And then I fell asleep. Ah, can I tell
The enchantment that afterwards befel?
Yet it was but a dream: yet such a dream
That never tongue, although it overteem
With mellow utterance, like a cavern spring,
Could figure out and to conception bring
All I beheld and felt.

To recover the dream in his waking state, to convert the ethereal perfection to an eternal reality, Endymion moves increasingly through rich entanglements, enthrallments self-destroying. Through his intensive imaginative pursuit, he hopes to melt into the radiance of the chief intensity.

With Kafka, the world of visions is a world of no return. In the mirror of inner-time, one can reach out only to self; and the reflection is always too hard, too cold, and ultimately too shattering. But for Endymion, as for all mortals within the Keatsian world, there must always be a return to clock-time, a tolling back to sole self, to fast-fading violets and "the coming musk-rose, full of dewy wine."

ODE TO A
NIGHTINGALE, *V*

TO J. H. REYNOLDS,
*82–5*

—It is a flaw
In happiness to see beyond our bourn—
It forces us in Summer skies to mourn:
It spoils the singing of the Nightingale.

ENDYMION,
*I, 453–61*

In *Sleep and Poetry* as well as in *Endymion,* "magic sleep" is not just the initial rung on the hierarchical ladder of values; it is also the "great key to golden palaces," opening those chambers beyond which are housed our innermost thoughts and feelings. It makes possible the imaginative projection which

transports us beyond our person into a maze of silver enchantment. By removing us from real things which, like a muddy
stream, would bear along our souls to nothingness, sleep would
dissolve the restrictive confines of things and self, inducing the
workings of the sympathetic imagination. It offers a balm to a
world "full of Misery and Heartbreak, Pain, Sickness and op-     *Ltr. to Reynolds,*
pression." It eases the way into the life ethereal. Unlike Words-  *3 May 1818*
worth, we can be released from the dark and misty passages
leading out from the Chamber of Maiden Thought. With "the
poppied warmth of sleep," one can, like Madeline, be "bliss-     THE EVE OF ST.
fully haven'd both from joy and pain; /. . . Blinded alike        AGNES, *XXVII*
from sunshine and from rain." Holding out a promise, the
imagination lulls us into that state where all we know and need   ODE ON A
to know is that beauty is truth, truth beauty:                    GRECIAN URN, *V*

> O soft embalmer of the still midnight,                          TO SLEEP
>     Shutting, with careful fingers and benign,
> Our gloom-pleas'd eyes, embower'd from the light,
>     Enshaded in forgetfulness divine;
> O soothest Sleep! if so it please thee, close,
>     In midst of this thine hymn, my willing eyes,
> Or wait the amen, ere thy poppy throws
>     Around my bed its lulling charities;
>     Then save me, or the passed day will shine
> Upon my pillow, breeding many woes;
>     Save me from curious conscience, that still lords
> Its strength for darkness, burrowing like a mole;
>     Turn the key deftly in the oiled wards,
> And seal the hushed casket of my soul.

Not all indolence and dreams are a good, however. The
ascetic beadsman in *The Eve of St. Agnes* dreams of a heaven
without sensations; the two brothers in *Isabella* have visions of
money, of gold and silver; the knight in *La Belle Dame Sans
Merci,* still in the thrall of a visionary lady in the meads, must
sojourn, haggard and woe-begone,

> Alone and palely loitering,                                     LA BELLE DAME
>     Though the sedge has wither'd from the lake,                 SANS MERCI, *XII*
>     And no birds sing.

TO J. H. REYNOLDS,
67–71 The imagination can turn in upon itself, shadowing "our own Soul's day-time / In the dark void of Night." It may never get beyond the weariness, the fever and the fret. In his epistle to Reynolds Keats urges:

> O that our dreamings all of sleep or wake
> Would all their colours from the Sunset take:
> From something of material sublime.

Like a muddy stream, the imagination turned in upon itself would bear along our soul to nothingness. The imagination SLEEP AND POETRY,
81–4 must be strong enough to seize the things and events of the wide world, to pursue sublime materials, to tease the spirit with their promise, "Till at its shoulders it should proudly see / Wings to find out an immortality."

"Fanatics have their dreams," Keats reminds us at the opening of *The Fall of Hyperion*. The savage also reaches from his sleep for the things of heaven. But without the creative imagination, without sympathy, these men only live and dream THE FALL OF
HYPERION, *I*,
199–202 and die. This is why "the poet and the dreamer are distinct, / Diverse, sheer opposite, antipodes." While the poet pours out his balm upon the world, the mere dreamer only vexes it. Without the creative act, without the telling of dreams, without poetry to cast its own spell, the imagination cannot be saved from dumb enchantment:

THE FALL OF
HYPERION, *I, 1–18*

> Fanatics have their dreams, wherewith they weave
> A paradise for a sect; the savage too
> From forth the loftiest fashion of his sleep
> Guesses at Heaven: pity these have not
> Trac'd upon vellum or wild indian leaf
> The shadows of melodious utterance.
> But bare of laurel they live, dream and die;
> For Poesy alone can tell her dreams,
> With the fine spell of words alone can save
> Imagination from the sable charm
> And dumb enchantment. Who alive can say
> 'Thou art no Poet; mayst not tell thy dreams'?
> . . . Every man whose soul is not a clod

Hath visions, and would speak, if he had lov'd
And been well nurtured in his mother tongue . . .

For George and Georgiana, Keats describes the "great difference between an easy and an uneasy indolence":

—An indolent day—fill'd with speculations even of an unpleasant colour
—is bearable and even pleasant alone—when one's thoughts cannot find
out any thing better in the world; and experience has told us that
locomotion is no change: but to have nothing to do, and to be surrounded
with unpleasant human identities; who press upon one just enough to
prevent one getting into a lazy position; and not enough to interest or
rouse one; is a capital punishment of a capital crime: for is not giving up,
through good nature, one's time to people who have no light and shade a
capital crime?

*Ltr. to George &
Georgiana,
17 Mar. 1819*

Like dreams that only "shadow our own soul's day-time," an
uneasy indolence can inhibit the powers of the creative imagination. Far from creating our identities, it would destroy us.
But there are other deterrents, some still greater, that can drag
our souls to nothingness.

Age, maturity, experience are all essential ingredients in the
creation of a soul. Unfortunately, youth and immaturity prevent our being carried beyond our own person. The egotism of
childhood, like that of the savage and the fanatic, is incapable
of forming in its imagination any conception of another man's
sensations. Of his fifteen year old sister, Keats comments, "her
character is not formed; her identity does not press upon me.
. . ." As with other children in general, he recognizes that their
death can only indicate a return of their spark or intelligence
to its divine source, "without any identity—it having had no
time to learn of, and be altered by, the heart. . . ." At the age
of twenty-three, he himself lacks a complete identity and is
therefore without the necessary means for fullest creativity. On
surveying the Elgin Marbles, he is fully persuaded that he must
die "like a sick Eagle looking at the sky," for his "spirit is too
weak—mortality / Weighs heavily" upon him. "Haydon! forgive me," he writes in the accompanying sonnet, "Forgive me
that I have not Eagle's wings— / That what I want I know not
where to seek." Growing "wings to find out an immortality" is

*Ltr. to George &
Georgiana,
14 Oct. 1818*

*Ltr. to George &
Georgiana,
21 Apr. 1819*

ON SEEING THE
ELGIN MARBLES

TO B. R. HAYDON

SLEEP AND POETRY,
*84*

Ltr. to Bailey,
10 June 1818

apparently not a child's task. To Bailey, Keats can lament his being "not old enough or magnanimous enough to annihilate self"; and three months later, he confesses this same failing to Dilke. Depressed at the illness of his brother, Keats himself is flung into "a continual fever—it must be poisonous to life although I feel well . . . I really have not self possession and magnanimity enough. . . ."

Ltr. to Dilke,
21 Sept. 1818

Ltr. to Woodhouse,
27 Oct. 1818

He himself may lack complete magnanimity; yet "the words-worthian or egotistical sublime; which is a thing per se and stands alone" is still more to be lamented as a deterrent for the sympathetic imagination. Instead of a life of sensations, men are offered by modern egotists a life of thought. Increasingly, we find ourselves with modern poets "bullied into a certain Philosophy engendered in the whims of an Egotist—Every man has his speculations, but every man does not brood and peacock over them till he makes a false coinage and deceives himself." Why be teased with the grandeur of Wordsworth or the merits of Leigh Hunt, when we can have poetry uncontaminated and unobtrusive? Why kick against the pricks, when we can be walking on roses?

Ltr. to Reynolds,
3 Feb. 1818

> Poetry should be great & unobtrusive, a thing which enters into one's soul, and does not startle it or amaze it with itself but with its subject.—How beautiful are the retired flowers! how would they lose their beauty were they to throng into the highway crying out, "admire me I am a violet! dote upon me I am a primrose!"

Clearly, love of one's own speculations, one's logic, one's truth, is love misapplied. It moves us inwardly, rather than outwardly. It strives to maintain isolation and self-identity, rather than to seek from interaction with the world external to self a means to create an identity, a soul.

Not until the end of the nineteenth century, with Ivan Karamazov and Raskolnikov, those great "doubles" of Dostoevsky, do these Keatsian apprehensions about the "egotistical sublime" develop major proportions. A reaching after truth, contrived only within the confines of their own intellect, reinforces in both Ivan and Raskolnikov the greatest individualism—and the greatest hell. Instead of self-realization, they arrive at complete solitude. The force of their own intellect has split them

apart from others. Logic has kept them each within his own groove, holding them aloof. They attain not fullness of life, but self-destruction; not social solidarity, but isolation. For Keats, as for Dostoevsky, they must be seen as "the worst of Men . . . whose self interests are their passion." *Ltr. to Georgiana, 15 Jan. 1820*

The lesson of St. John—"Except a corn of wheat fall into the ground and die, it abideth alone: but if it die, it bringeth forth much fruit"—is offered in turn by Father Zossima to the mysterious visitor who attends him during his own youth, and again to the young novice Alyosha. This is the theme offered by Dostoevsky to his reader through the opening inscription for *Brothers Karamazov.* Like Endymion who must wreathe a flowery band to bind him to the earth, Alyosha must fall upon the ground and water it with his tears, vowing passionately to love it forever and forever, just as Raskolnikov must confess his crime at the lonely crossroads, kissing the earth in symbolic confession of his own mortality. Unlike Dimitri who would cling forever to the earth, but needs a blow of fate to save him from his sensual degradation, and unlike Ivan who will not pay the price, Alyosha can begin to bring forth much fruit. He shares the Keatsian recognition that

> The flower must drink the nature of the soil          SPENSER!
> Before it can put forth its blossoming.

He has accepted the stench of human corruption, the putrefaction of Zossima's body, as well as his own. And from this must arise sympathy, not egotism; a brotherhood of boys, and not the guilt of self-isolation. As in Keats's world, love in Dostoevsky is clearly the antithesis of logic, not of hate; and soul is an enemy of solitude.

For the Russian novelist, however, love for humanity is predicated upon the edifice of Christ. Any other edifice is a tower of Babel, built by those demi-gods who demand happiness upon earth. But Keats, steeped in the neo-humanism of the early nineteenth century and intent upon the power of his second deity to form "greater things than our Creator himself made," *Ltr. to Haydon, 10–11 May 1817* would encourage, and without the assistance of religion, a search for earthly happiness. In Dostoevsky the Grand Inquisi-

tor can juxtapose man's demand for earthly bread and the heavenly bread promised to the meek at the close of earthly time-dimensions; but in Keats, the spiritual is attainable only through the material; the heavenly, only through the mortal. Through sympathy, through love and compassion, the chameleon poet bridges the gap between inner self and outer being. He uses the sympathetic imagination almost as an intuitive and biological faculty to achieve social solidarity and the brotherhood of man. For Keats, it is the only means by which man can create for himself an identity—through the *act* of love, rather than the *spirit* of love.

*Ltr. to George & Georgiana, 17 Dec. 1818*

Thus, with "vain, egotistical" Leigh Hunt, Keats recognizes a singular grasp of beauty. Yet, Hunt makes "fine things petty and beautiful things hateful . . . and many a glorious thing when associated with him becomes a nothing." And expressing his apprehensions about Endymion's pursuit of the immortal Cynthia, Keats is aware that the greatest threats are "thoughts of self," the failure of the empathic pursuit, "the journey homeward to habitual self" through nettled briars and tangled swamps.

ENDYMION, *II, 274–80*

*Ltr. to George & Georgiana, 19 Mar. 1819*

And yet, "very few men have ever arrived at a complete disinterestedness of Mind," Keats is quick to concede:

. . . very few have been influenced by a pure desire of the benefit of others —in the greater part of the Benefactors [of] & to Humanity some meretricious motive has sullied their greatness—some melodramatic scenery has fascinated them. . . . I perceive how far I am from any humble standard of disinterestedness.

In all history, he can recall but two men, Socrates and Jesus, who succeeded in annihilating the self by developing "hearts completely disinterested." True, if this principle of disinterestedness were carried to its highest pitch in wild nature, the lion as well as the swallow would starve. We wander in society with much the same instinctiveness; still there can be little fear of injury to men by instituting this principle. What differentiates mortals from the lion as well as the swallow is the sympathetic imagination, acting as "an ellectric fire in human nature tending to purify—so that among these human creatures there is continually some birth of new heroism."

The struggle within himself is perpetual. "One is nothing— *Ltr. to Woodhouse,*
Perhaps I eat to persuade myself I am somebody." Although the  *21 Sept. 1819*
body may insist on being a "somebody," consciousness pulls in
quite the contrary direction: "I am obliged continually to  *Ltr. to Reynolds,*
check myself and strive to be nothing."  *24 Aug. 1819*

Yet another deterrent for the sympathetic imagination—as
much within the nature of mortality as youth and egotism—is
death. It threatens to move us out of human time, out of the
life of sensations.

To the casual reader, Keats's views on death appear strangely
ambivalent. In the *Ode to a Nightingale,* even while the singer
is "half in love with easeful Death" and feels it "rich to die," he
also emulates the immortal bird who was born for death.
Beginning with an intensive pursuit of the timelessness repre-
sented by the bird, he yearns for self-annihilation that would
move him outside of time. Initially, the singer would abandon
mortality, the mutations of man caught within the imprisoning
web of clock-time, "where youth grows pale and spectre-thin,
and dies." Like Quentin in Faulkner's *The Sound and the
Fury,* he is worn away by a minute clicking of little wheels, by a
mechanical progression within a world "where Beauty cannot keep her lustrous eyes." Ultimately, he comes to recognize that timelessness is inconsonant with mortality, for it
threatens the end of sensation. "To cease upon the midnight
with no pain" is to "have ears in vain," becoming a sod to the
high requiem of the bird. And so, within the context of the ode,
as within the larger context of the letters and the poetry, ambiv-
alences recede and disparities melt away into nothingness.

Man may be born for death, yet through his pursuit of the
things of beauty, embodied here in the bird's song, the mortal
songster can find for himself an immortality. By sympathetic
interaction with the bird, through the "viewless wings of
Poesy," he can produce an ode. Through his own poetry, he
adds a mite, as it were, to the singing of the nightingale. Yet, to
pursue with totality the essence of the bird's song is to annihilate with utter abandon one's own self, one's ode-making self, to
denigrate the world of sensations so crucial for the creative
act. Because the creative act must be perpetual, the sympathetic

imagination must have the daily supply of sensations. The human heart and mind must interact in the world of elemental space, an interaction so essential to school a soul. Complete projection of self through the imagination would mean complete annihilation; therefore, only so much of the annihilating process is desirable, and no more. Unless the singer in the ode is tolled back to his sole self, interaction of self with the world is no longer possible. Self becomes a has-been; the ode becomes a might-have-been. The potentialities of the present are then annihilated.

Seemingly, only a thin dividing line separates the mortal world from the non-mortal. Defined within the structure of the ode, the singer's goal is not immortality. It is rather the process of moving through mortality up to, but no further than, that thin dividing line, beyond which lies the embalmed darkness of death. Understandably, the singer in the ode is only "half in love" with death: enough to provide some measure of self-annihilation, but not so much that there can be no return and the beginning of new sensations, new creative acts, new experiences, new odes, that will go into the making of an identity. From the beginning, Endymion is cautioned by the aged priest of the "fragile bar / That keeps us from our homes ethereal." Before long, a nymph will rise from the fountain's lilies to warn the imprudent shepherd:

ENDYMION,
I, 360–1

ENDYMION,
II, 123–7

>             . . . thou must wander far
> In other regions, past the scanty bar
> To mortal steps, before thou cans't be ta'en
> From every wasting sigh, from every pain,
> Into the gentle bosom of thy love.

ENDYMION,
III, 315–6

Even Glaucus points to his own tragedy, that his "soul stands / Now past the midway from mortality." By the close of the narrative, Endymion himself has learned this lesson. To pursue beyond the scanty bar the immortality symbolized by Cynthia is to annihilate self with totality. To cease upon the midnight with no pain is also to end the creative process, the life of sensations through which one can carve his identity. Now, he himself is ready to confess:

> There never liv'd a mortal man, who bent
> His appetite beyond his natural sphere,
> But starv'd and died.

ENDYMION,
*IV, 646–8*

A complete melting and blending into oneness, a total "fellowship with essence," may appear as the ideal toward which one strives in his search for happiness. It is the means, the only means to create one's identity. Still, the ardent pursuer, moving through the world of sensations, must look upon this essence more as an aim than a goal. It is more a direction to be pursued than a prize to be won. To capture the prize is, paradoxically, to lose it. To win the race is self-defeating, for then men must forget their mortal way:

> Scanty the hour and few the steps beyond the bourn of care,
> Beyond the sweet and bitter world,—beyond it unaware!
> Scanty the hour and few the steps, because a longer stay
> Would bar return, and make a man forget his mortal way.

LINES WRITTEN IN
THE HIGHLANDS,
*29–32*

Though one should pursue immortality, the sympathetic imagination must never forget its mortal condition—the flowery band that binds it to earth, making possible, to the highest degree, an intensity of pursuit. "I wish for death every day and night to deliver me from these pains," Keats writes in one of his moving last letters, trembling within the same paradox, "and then I wish death away, for death would destroy even those pains which are better than nothing."

*Ltr. to Brown,
30 Sept. 1820*

The viewless wings of poesy may offer a greater degree of intensity than Bacchus and his pards, the realm of Flora and old Pan; but higher than verse, fame, and beauty is Death. It is the chief intensity, life's highest meed:

> Why did I laugh tonight? No voice will tell:
>   No God, no Demon of severe response,
> Deigns to reply from Heaven or from Hell.
>   Then to my human heart I turn at once.
> Heart! Thou and I are here sad and alone;
>   I say, why did I laugh? O mortal pain!
> O Darkness! Darkness! ever must I moan,

WHY DID I LAUGH

To question Heaven and Hell and Heart in vain.
Why did I laugh? I know this Being's lease,
  My fancy to its utmost blisses spreads;
Yet would I on this very midnight cease,
  And the world's gaudy ensigns see in shreds;
Verse, Fame, and Beauty are intense indeed,
But Death intenser—Death is Life's high meed.

Almost instinctively, the mortal creator longs to

SLEEP AND POETRY,                                die a death
          58-9
                  Of luxury, and my young spirit follow
                  The morning sun-beams to the great Apollo . . .

He finds that having

ODE TO A                        been half in love with easeful Death . . .
NIGHTINGALE, *VI*
                  Now more than ever seems it rich to die,
                  To cease upon the midnight with no pain . . .

He craves to stand

WHEN I HAVE FEARS                                         on the shore
                  Of the wide world . . . alone, and think
                  Till love and fame to nothingness do sink.

Like the knight in *La Belle Dame,* he yearns to be once again
within the thrall of the lady in the meads, the fairy child who
TO HOMER   sings a fairy's song. He longs to live, like Homer, where "on the
shores of darkness there is light," with "a budding morrow in
midnight" and "a triple sight in blindness keen." Yet, simultaneously there is the recognition that this highest of intensities is
paradoxical and self-defeating. Ultimately, it can only negate
the life of sensations.

It is understandable that Keats knowingly avoids complete
identification with his dying brother Tom:

*Ltr. to Dilke,*   His identity presses upon me so all day that I am obliged to go out. . . . I
*21 Sept. 1818*   am obliged to write, and plunge into abstract images to ease myself of his
countenance his voice and feebleness—so that I live now in a continual
fever—it must be poisonous to life although I feel well.

Mortality alone contains the seeds for our immortality. Only the things and materials of existence carry with them the possibilities of futurity, ever-fresh, ever-changing:

> Life is the rose's hope while yet unblown;
> The reading of an ever-changing tale;
> The light uplifting of a maiden's veil;
> A pigeon tumbling in clear summer air;
> A laughing school-boy, without grief or care,
> Riding the springy branches of an elm.

SLEEP AND POETRY,
90–5

Therefore, of necessity, we must bind ourselves to the earth, to the limited beauties and time-bound intensities of mortal existence, to the limited projections of the sympathetic imagination.

# 9
# Creative Technique: Negative Capability

*Ltr. to Bailey, 22 Nov. 1817*

When Bailey finally obtained his curacy late in 1817, Keats wrote to express his own certainty of "nothing but of the holiness of the Heart's affections and the truth of Imagination." Bailey's clerical position, far from inhibiting the anti-clerical Keats, seems to have helped in crystallizing the poet's own thoughts on theology. Only a few weeks earlier, Keats had

*Ltr. to Bailey, 3 Nov. 1817*

freely expressed to Bailey his longing "for a recourse somewhat human [and] independant of the great consolations of Religion." And before too many months, safe in the assurance that

*Ltr. to Bailey, 13 Mar. 1818*

"you know my ideas about Religion," Keats was explaining his vision of how our own minds can "consecrate whate'er they look upon," the *means* by which mortals without the assistance of a deity can transform the contents of the earth into greater dignity and worth. In his discourse on "the holiness of the Heart's affections," however, Keats's concern is with the *manner* of artistic representation—the techniques by which materials of mortal existence, pursued by means of the sympathetic imagination, can be translated into an art form:

*Ltr. to Bailey, 22 Nov. 1817*

I am certain of nothing but of the holiness of the Heart's affections and the truth of Imagination—What the imagination seizes as Beauty must be truth—whether it existed before or not—for I have the same Idea of all

our Passions as of Love they are all in their sublime, creative of essential Beauty—In a Word, you may know my favorite Speculation by my first Book [of *Endymion*] and the little song [*O Sorrow*] I sent in my last—which is a representation from the fancy of the probable mode of operating in these Matters—The Imagination may be compared to Adam's dream—he awoke and found it truth. I am the more zealous in this affair, because I have never yet been able to perceive how any thing can be known for truth by consequitive reasoning—and yet it must be—Can it be that even the greatest Philosopher ever arrived at his goal without putting aside numerous objections—However it may be, O for a Life of Sensations rather than of Thoughts! It is 'a Vision in the form of Youth' a Shadow of reality to come—and this consideration has further convinced me for it has come as auxiliary to another favorite Speculation of mine, that we shall enjoy ourselves here after by having what we called happiness of Earth repeated in a finer tone and so repeated—And yet such a fate can only befall those who delight in sensation rather than hunger as you do after Truth— Adam's dream will do here and seems to be a conviction that Imagination and its empyreal reflection is the same as human Life and its spiritual repetition. But as I was saying—the simple imaginative Mind may have its rewards in the repetition of its own silent Working coming continually on the Spirit with a fine suddenness. . . .

Keats's comparison of his own world of visions with Adam's dream can be curiously deceptive. In the eighth book of *Paradise Lost* Adam's dream emerges from a theocentric framework in which the powers of an omnipotent divinity and his relationship to man's will are resolutely expressed by Milton. When "he awoke and found it truth," Adam came to recognize that the mercies of a Christian God had afforded him with a prefigurement of "reality to come."

Despite the absence of a Christian deity in Aristotle's two treatises—*On Dreams* and *On Prophesying by Dreams*—the dreamwork appears equally prophetic. A movement set up first in sleep may well prove the starting point of action performed in the daytime. Yet, Aristotle recognizes that the recurrence of thoughts or deeds by day may well have been prepared for by images of the mind at night. Even within Aristotle's classical framework, the dream is not coincident with Keats's "Shadow of reality to come," though for Aristotle the "reality" is only a development of potentialities explored during the sleeping hours, and the dreamwork an early confrontation with choices.

From the twentieth-century perspective, dreams can afford

no less "a Shadow of reality to come." Through dreams, we are enabled to discover the dispositions of the libido and the realities of a repressed unconscious. Freud suggests that the condition of sleep produces a certain relaxation of repression, so that forms assumed by wish-fulfillment within the framework of dreams can reveal objects to which the libido has attached itself. The ultimate referent, that through which the symbolism assumes its meaning and by which it is given its form, is always the particular psyche of the dreamer himself. Unlike Adam, if the modern dreamer is to wake and find it "truth," he must through his own devices make it self-fulfilling rather than self-repressing.

The dream theories of Freud are not at work with Keats any more than are the theories of Aristotle. But the supernatural framework of Milton is equally an anathema for the early nineteenth-century poet. Freud and Aristotle are both too highly dependent upon analytic thought for the repetition in a finer tone of the shadowed world of visions; and Milton is too independent of man's mortal powers, particularly sympathy and the life of sensations upon which the imagination is dependent.

With Keats, visions are sometimes wholly prophetic, like this dream to which he alludes in the letter to Bailey. Hermes has in LAMIA, *Lamia* an early vision of his sweet nymph by the river. And *I, 68–80* Lamia herself has had a splendid dream of Hermes, abandoning his golden throne and striking for her Cretan isle in sad HYPERION, search of the invisible maid. In *Hyperion* Apollo dreams of *III, 50–67* Mnemosyne, even before he finds her and a golden lyre beside him in the forest. But Hermes, Lamia, and Apollo are not LAMIA, *I, 127* mortal. "Real are the dreams of Gods," we are assured, but mortals must pursue their dreams with an ardent intensity to stamp them with reality and worth. At best, a mortal's dream in Keats can only be partially prophetic. Endymion dreams of Cynthia. Isabella has her vision of Lorenzo, a "pale shadow" with "cold doom / Upon his lips," dwelling alone upon the fringe of human nature. The knight-at-arms in *La Belle Dame* has a dream within a dream, a vision of the faery lady in the meads who draws him to an elfin grot for sleep, where he can dream of death-pale warriors and princes pale. With each, the

dreamer must pursue his vision during his waking state in order to make it "truth," the "Shadow of reality to come."

So too with Madeline's dream of Porphyro in *The Eve of St. Agnes*. Having retired to her chamber on this St. Agnes eve, when legend promises that dreams of mortals can foretell a truth, Madeline performs the ceremonies proper to assure a vision of her lover. But Porphyro, impatient in his burning, steals into her rooms to waken her with ancient ditties played upon a hollow lute:

> Her eyes were open, but she still beheld,
> Now wide awake, the vision of her sleep:
> There was a painful change, that nigh expell'd
> The blisses of her dream so pure and deep
> At which fair Madeline began to weep,
> And moan forth witless words with many a sigh;
> While still her gaze on Porphyro would keep;
> Who knelt, with joined hands and piteous eye,
> Fearing to move or speak, she look'd so dreamingly.

THE EVE OF ST. AGNES, *XXXIV–XXXV*

> 'Ah, Porphyro!' said she, 'but even now
> 'Thy voice was at sweet tremble in mine ear,
> 'Made tuneable with every sweetest vow;
> 'And those sad eyes were spiritual and clear:
> 'How chang'd thou art! how pallid, chill, and drear!
> 'Give me that voice again, my Porphyro,
> 'Those looks immortal, those complainings dear!
> 'Oh leave me not in this eternal woe,
> 'For if thou diest, my Love, I know not where to go.'

The prophetic quality of Madeline's dream, like that of any mortal—Endymion, Isabella, the knight of *La Belle Dame*—is only partially fulfilled. Awake, she can detect a "painful change" between the blissful vision of her dream with "looks immortal" and her waking apprehension of a lover "pallid, chill, and drear." Before, in her imaginative apprehension of beauty, her lover's eyes were "spiritual and clear," his voice "at sweet tremble" in her ear. Like the figure on the Grecian urn, the lover of her dreams might love forever, singing his melo-

dies, not to her sensual ear, but to her spirit. Awakened from her azure-lidded sleep and confronted by a mortal lover, Madeline sighs at once: "How chang'd thou art!"

When Milton's Adam awakens from his rest, he is, of course, confronted by no such alteration, his dream having been infiltrated and guided throughout by an omnipotent and omniscient deity. He awakens to discover only a replica of what he has been promised. God has, as it were, fulfilled in the waking world what has been promised in the world of visions. In a sense, Madeline's dream has also offered her a promise. But hers is only the "Shadow of a reality to come." Her mortal lover in the world of pains and annoyances is only a shadow of the ideal lover in her vision: paler, colder, drearier. To merge these two visions, the mortal and the immortal, she must pursue with intensity the one through the other during her waking state. Of a "no thing" she must create a "thing real."

This same problem confronts the dreamer in *La Belle Dame.* The victim of a dream within a dream, he has a vision of a "lady in the meads" who leads him on through rich entanglements to a dream of death-pale warriors crying, "La Belle Dame sans Merci / Hath thee in thrall!" An imaginative pursuit of this vision during his waking state can move him only into complete self-annihilation. And so, haggard and woe-begone, poised at the midnight point between light and darkness, the sign of death upon his fevered brow, he palely loiters on the cold hillside, where

> The sedge has wither'd from the lake,
> And no birds sing.

Set off from this pursuit of a distinctive love *sans merci,* Madeline's vision opens the way to greatest fulfillment. By an intensive and fevered pursuit through the imagination, essential beauty can become a truth, whether or not it was so initially. Not Porphyro himself, corporeal and substantive, but her imaginative vision of Porphyro is sublime and creative of essential beauty. Only if the vision is pursued through "a Life of Sensations, rather than Thoughts," however, can it produce essential beauty. Because Porphyro shares with her

an ethereal vision, having himself pursued her with passionate THE EVE OF
ST. AGNES,
X, XIII intensity even within the sanctity of her chambers, his own imagination can blend with hers. She has already stormed "his heart, Love's fev'rous citadel." Therefore, he invades the outer portals of the castle, "pale, lattic'd, chill, and silent as a tomb." Before long, he penetrates the middle chamber of her thought. Ltr. to Reynolds,
3 May 1818 Soon, he will pursue her in the inner chamber of her soul. By melting into her dream, he can fulfill the promise:

> Beyond a mortal man impassion'd far THE EVE OF ST.
AGNES,
XXXVI
> At these voluptuous accents, he arose,
> Ethereal, flush'd, and like a throbbing star
> Seen mid the sapphire heaven's deep repose
> Into her dream he melted, as the rose
> Blendeth its odour with the violet . . .

Thus, the mutual pursuit, the interaction initiated within a life of sensations, offers a fulfillment of the promise held out by the "shadow of reality." The limited happiness available through sensations can be repeated in the world of the imagination through a finer tone. Like Endymion, the two lovers would find their happiness in that which beckons their ready minds to fellowship divine; in the end, their souls can interknit and mingle, blending into the radiance of one another. Like Endymion's dream of Cynthia, Madeline's dream of Porphyro is "a Shadow of reality to come." Without the ardent pursuit, the shadow must remain a "no thing." Only through "its spiritual repetition," by repeatedly and infinitely annihilating the self in pursuit of rich entanglements and enthrallments self-destroying, can human minds and hearts create a soul to enjoy the fullest degree of happiness.

Thus, when Porphyro and Madeline melt into one another's dreams, fleeing into the storm, they are offered a fulfillment of life's highest meed. "Real are the dreams of Gods," but the LAMIA, I, 127 dreams of mortal men can be equally real—if they are pursued. To pursue with the greatest intensity the things of beauty within this bittersweet world of fever and of fret is to cease upon the midnight with no pain, to abandon the world of sensations. Porphyro and Madeline, fleeing into the "elfin storm

THE EVE OF   from faery land," speed into the realm where "there are no ears
ST. AGNES,   to hear, or eyes to see." They move out of the world of human
*XXXIX*   time, beyond the mortal realm of sensations. They cease "on
WHY DID I LAUGH   this very midnight," henceforth to live only in the legendary
land of poetry and romance. But for mortal man—for Endy-
mion, for the lonely sojourner of *La Belle Dame,* for the singer
of the nightingale ode—there must always be a bell, tolling him
back from faery lands forlorn. Within the human condition

TO J. H. REYNOLDS,                         it is a flaw
*82–5*               In happiness to see beyond our bourn
It forces us in Summer skies to mourn:
It spoils the singing of the Nightingale.

To the degree that it holds forth a promise which we ourselves can in our waking state fulfill, "Adam's dream will do
here" then, for "the simple imaginative Mind may have its
rewards in the repetition of its own silent Working." The
limited truth to which we awaken in this mortal world of pain
and annoyances, the weariness and fret that must alternate
with our vision of eternal beauty, will suffice. It will suffice,
because "what the imagination seizes as Beauty must be truth."
It must be, because there is no other truth that we can apprehend. It will suffice, because truth is not really the concern of
our dreams. Nor is it really the concern of those sensations
which have given rise to dreams. At best, we must concern
ourselves here only with the seizure of beauty in all *its* truth,
with the pursuit of sensations in all *their* truth, whether that
truth existed before or not. As long as men can wreathe the
flowery band that ties them to the earth, struggling through
"all our Passions as of Love," then happiness eternally, joy
forever which is "creative of essential beauty," can be known.

Nothing then "can be known for a truth by consequitive
reasoning," as Keats explains to Bailey in that letter on Adam's
dream. The alternatives are clearly defined. Even the greatest
philosophers have reached their goals only by "putting aside
numerous objections," thrusting from them the shackling inhi-
bition of reason. But the creation of poetry, like the creation of
an identity, is clearly evolved from a "life of sensations." Hap-

piness in a finer tone can only befall those delighting in sensations rather than hungering after truth. Like Wordsworth, or
like Dilke who "will never come at a truth as long as he lives;
because he is always trying at it," one who pursues knowledge
directly through his head alone will never find either truth or
joy. All we know—and indeed, all we need to know in this vale
of soul-making—is that beauty is its own truth, offering within
the perpetuity of time an eternal source of human happiness.

Thus, the silent form of the Grecian urn does "tease us out of ODE ON A
thought," insistent that beauty is its own truth. Before the GRECIAN URN, *V*
beauty of the urn, the antinomies of beauty and truth, life and
death, time and eternality, mortality and divinity—those intellectual antitheses which would tease us *into* thought—melt
away into nothingness. The urn in all its beauty remains:

> When old age shall this generation waste,
>   Thou shalt remain, in midst of other woe
> Than ours, a friend to man, to whom thou say'st,
>   Beauty is truth, truth beauty,—that is all
>   Ye know on earth, and all ye need to know.

Just as the urn, defiant of chronological time, remains to "tease
us out of thought / As doth eternity," the beauties of the ode
itself "remain, in midst of other woe." The writing of the ode,
like the making of the urn, is dedicated to saying that "Beauty
is truth, truth beauty." That the ode says this still, a century
and a half after its composition, "is all / Ye know on earth, and
all ye need to know."

In *Epistle IX,* Boileau had insisted with equal conviction
upon the direct contrary:

> *Rien n'est beau que le vrai: le vrai seul est aimable;*
> *Il doit régnet partout, et même dans la fable . . .*
> [Nothing is beautiful unless it is true: only the true
> is pleasant; it should reign everywhere, even in myth . . .]

For Boileau, as for much of the Age of "Reason," truth is more
important than beauty. In reversing this claim, Keats was to
recognize that "with a great poet the sense of Beauty overcomes

every other consideration." Accepting the world of beauty and quelling all hungers after truth—these are the cardinal qualities that the great poet must develop. Shakespeare possessed these qualities, as Keats was to point out; Coleridge lacked them. For Keats, certainly, Boileau lacked these qualities also.

The letter on Adam's dream had dwelt upon the relationship between truth and beauty, inherent within the techniques of *Ltr. to George &* true creativity. In a conversation with Dilke a few weeks later *Tom,* *21 Dec. 1817* the idea became all the more lucid. "Several things dovetailed in my mind," Keats begins:

> & at once it struck me, what quality went to form a Man of Achievement especially in Literature & which Shakespeare possessed so enormously—I mean *Negative Capability,* that is when man is capable of being in uncertainties, Mysteries, doubts, without any irritable reaching after fact & reason—Coleridge, for instance, would let go by a fine isolated verisimilitude caught from the Penetralium of mystery, from being incapable of remaining content with half knowledge. . . . with a great poet the sense of Beauty overcomes every other consideration, or rather obliterates all consideration.

"Negative Capability" is not to be confused in Keats with the "Sympathetic Imagination." The imagination is the *means* by which a mortal can step into a oneness. "Negative Capability" provides the *manner* through which the imaginative stepping can be creatively productive. It is the capacity for being in "uncertainties, mysteries, doubts." It is that quality which goes to "form a Man of Achievement especially in Literature." The creative artist must possess an essential capacity for being content with the "life of sensations rather than of thoughts." He must be satisfied to operate wholly within the "shadow of reality to come" and content himself to "delight in sensation rather than hunger . . . after Truth." He must recognize that "Adam's dream will do here," in this mortal state where the imagination and the holiness of the heart's affections are more rewarding than any irritable reaching by the intelligence after truths. "Things cannot to the will / Be settled, but they tease us out of thought," Keats assures us in the epistle to Reynolds. And in *Endymion,* hymns sung to sensuous Pan glorify the god:

> the unimaginable lodge
> For solitary thinkings; such as dodge
> Conception to the very bourne of heaven,
> Then leave the naked brain . . .

ENDYMION, I, 293–6

Because "the dull brain perplexes and retards," the things of beauty—a Grecian urn or the wailful choir of small gnats mourning—serve us well, if they do "tease us out of thought" and let us dodge conception. Not mind alone, but the interaction of heart and mind within the world of elemental space is essential, if men are to bear the stamp of an identity.

# 10

# Creative Technique:
# Truth and the Intellect

Keats's "Negative Capability" has sometimes been identified with Wordsworth's concept of "wise passiveness," but these two poetic theories are quite distinct. Wordsworth's poetic ends may involve pleasure or happiness, but "pleasure" for Wordsworth is intrinsically bound up with a search for epistemological truths. It partakes of knowledge and higher reason—of "Wisdom and Spirit of the universe," of "Reason in her most exalted mood," as the concept is expanded in *The Prelude*.

In his preface to *Lyrical Ballads,* Wordsworth had outlined a relatively clear exposition of how poetry aims at pleasure, "true pleasure [being] that which partakes of knowledge and higher reason." To arrive at this pleasurable end, the poet chooses incidents and situations, especially those which can give rise to powerful feelings. The "principal objects of imitation," he explains, are "situations from common life." Characters and events are chosen from "humble and rustic life," for in this simpler state are to be found "the most beautiful and permanent forms of nature." Here, "the essential passions of the heart find a better soil." But sensations represent only the initial half of Wordsworth's artistic experience. Having engaged in powerful feelings, indulged the passions through an interaction of self

with external reality, the poet must complete the experience through a creative act. This second half of the artistic experience is achieved by Wordsworth during a state of tranquility, when the original emotion is recollected in the state of association. Then, sensation is displaced by the sympathetic imagination. "The primary laws of our nature" are realized, but only by an imaginative projection over these objects and events as they are present in our minds, our memories, our associations. Then, the particular is properly subordinated to the universal, the transient to the permanent and indestructible, the passing passion to permanent laws. As Wordsworth explains the process in *Tintern Abbey,* it is only

> with an eye made quiet by the power
> Of harmony and the deep power of joy,
> We see into the life of things.

Thus, Wordsworth's famous definition of good poetry as "the spontaneous overflow of powerful feelings" is misleading, unless it is taken in his context which provides for an eventual subordination of feelings to "the primary laws of our nature." Although the overflow may be quite spontaneous initially, the creative act ensues only when the mind displaces feeling during the passive, associative state:

. . . All good poetry is the spontaneous overflow of powerful feelings: and though this be true, Poems to which any value can be attached were never produced on any variety of subjects but by a man who, being possessed of more than usual organic sensibility, had also thought long and deeply.

The poet "considers man and the objects that surround him as acting and reacting upon each other," but the passions must eventually be filtered through the synthetic powers of the imagination. Only then can subject and object interact on the highest level. Sensation is an essential preliminary to higher thoughts about the permanent and indestructible laws, the wisdom and spirit of the universe, reason in her most exalted mood. But eventually feelings are subordinated to truth. These truths can be known only through an initial sensorial state, through an experience with the world of things. But with

Wordsworth, passivity or indolence does not refine the sensation, as with Keats; it empties us of the particular. Transcend-
ing the mundane world of things, we are moved into their
higher spirit, into "the beauteous forms of things":

> One impulse from a vernal wood
> Can teach you more of man,
> Of moral evil and of good,
> Than all the sages can.
>
> Sweet is the lore which Nature brings;
> Our meddling intellect
> Mis-shapes the beauteous forms of things:—
> We murder to dissect.

By avoiding the analytic and dissecting powers of the intellect,
emphasizing instead its synthetic and associative powers,
Wordsworth is enabled to open the way for "certain inherent
and indestructible qualities of the human mind." These bear
upon "certain powers in the great and permanent objects that
act upon it, which are equally inherent and indestructible," as
he explains in his preface.

Keats obviously shares with Wordsworth a distrust of the
intellect as a meddling dissector. But Wordsworth lacks Keats's
negative capability, the capacity to be content with uncertainties, mysteries, doubts, the capacity to rest content with the
world of sensations. The vernal wood teases Wordsworth, not
out of thought, but directly into thought. It moves him into
moral evil and good, the higher thought than that which
might ensue from meddling and dissecting intellect. But impulse alone is insufficient for Wordsworth. In a state of "wise
passiveness," the "inward eye" deposes the outer eye which had
been limited to a particular impression, as in *I Wandered
Lonely As a Cloud*. When this is done, universal laws can be
viewed in all their truth. Like Wordsworth, Keats seeks his
poetic pleasures through an interaction of self and the external.
But Wordsworth's structuring of the poetic act (like his structuring of the metaphysical universe) is dependent upon his
transcendence of the world of things into the truths they can
teach us. Keats would structure the act on the basis of his

penetration into the essence of things. He would move through
and with them, and not above and beyond them. Like the
speaker in *The Fall of Hyperion,* Keats would grow a power

THE FALL OF
HYPERION, *I, 302–6*

> of enormous ken
> To see as a God sees, and take the depth
> Of things as nimbly as the outward eye
> Can size and shape pervade.

Initially, Keats's experience with the nightingale and Wordsworth's with a cuckoo have much in common. Wordsworth's
poem opens with an obvious dualism of poet and bird, subject
and object. The bird's voice is heard, as it has been heard in his
boyhood, as a very real, substantial thing. Previously, he had
sought to reinforce the audial experience with the visual,
searching for the substantive bird in bush, in tree, in sky,
seeking it in woods and on the green. Now, lying supine upon
the grass, he hears again the cuckoo's shout passing from one
substantial hill to another. The difference between the boyhood experience and that of the mature poet is the development of "wise passiveness." Now he does not seek a corporeal
bird. Now he recognizes that it is not only "Bird, . . . but a
wandering Voice." It is "an invisible thing, a voice, a mystery."
The syncretising powers of the imagination have replaced the
original sensorial experience:

> . . . I can listen to thee yet;
> Can lie upon the plain
> And listen, till I do beget
> That golden time again.
>
> O blessed Bird! the earth we pace
> Again appears to be
> An unsubstantial, faery place;
> That is fit home for Thee!

By means of the bird, the world of hills and trees, woods and
sky, is transformed into "an unsubstantial, faery place."
Through the poet's wise passivity, the cuckoo itself is transformed. At first, the singer wonders whether he shall call it

"Bird, / Or but a wandering Voice." Once the associating powers of the imagination begin their work, he moves into a higher stage. He can affirm, "thou art to me / No bird, but an invisible thing, / A voice, a mystery. . . ." Before this brief poem has drawn to a close, the blithe newcomer and darling of the spring has been fully identified with the "Wisdom and Spirit of the universe." Now it is a "blessed Bird," hailed like a deity: a holy "Thou" rather than an estranged "it."

Wordsworth's procedure is not entirely unfamiliar. The interaction between subject and object, which succeeds through efforts of the sympathetic imagination in breaking down the isolation of the individual, is of course basic to Keats. But the poetic movement leads Wordsworth, unlike Keats, to an abandonment of the sensuous experience once higher truths are realized. By "purifying . . . the elements of feeling and of thought" and by "sanctifying, by such discipline," the poet may transform "the mean and vulgar works of man" into "high objects" and "enduring things"—as Wordsworth explains in the first book of *The Prelude*. In the transformation of bird to mystery, sunshine and flowers to "an unsubstantial faery place," the dramatic action is displaced by wise passivity. The poetic structure is made to coincide with a larger value system, as the substantive universe is transcended by the spiritual. As with Shelley, the Wordsworthian experience is dependent for its reality upon truths that exist only in an extra-mundane world outside of human time.

Wordsworth makes the same imaginative leap in *The Solitary Reaper,* where the creative imagination must move beyond the Highland lass singing in the vale. At first, she is only an object, a thing. To be truly creative, the associating mind must turn away from the particular and seek the universal. And so, before long, the girl herself is left far behind, reaping and singing by herself, as the poet in his state of "wise passiveness" listens

> motionless and still;
> And, as I mounted up the hill
> The music in my heart I bore,
> Long after it was heard no more.

The Highland lass is left behind, just as cuckoo as bird is transcended. Thing functions as symbol only insofar as it achieves an effect upon self, insofar as it can be used by self to reaffirm universal laws and higher truths.

Wordsworth's poetic movement is from the sensorial to the epistemological, from interaction to knowledge. Because of his emphasis upon universal truths, men and things have ultimate value for Wordsworth only insofar as their corporeality can be transcended. For Blake, on the contrary, things are themselves invested with value:

"What," it will be Question'd, "When the Sun rises, do you not see a round disk of fire somewhat like a Guinea?" O no, no, I see an Innumerable company of the Heavenly host crying, "Holy, Holy, Holy is the Lord God Almighty." I question not my Corporeal or Vegetable Eye any more than I would Question a Window concerning a Sight. I look thro' it & not with it.

Unlike Wordsworth's Highland lass who is transcended as girl, or his cuckoo purified of its dross as bird, Blake's sun *is* the "Heavenly host." It may appear as "a round disk of fire" to the 'Corporeal or Vegetable Eye"; but Blake's inner eye is not impeded by appearances. Wordsworth must displace the outer eye with the inner, and in the process displace thing with its truth; but Blake looks only with the inner eye and sees thing itself as truth. The sun *is* the heavenly host, just as man *is* divine. Eternality exists within every moment of human time.

Because the merry dancer in Blake's *The Crystal Cabinet* would strive, like Wordsworth, "to seize the inmost form," his joy is turned to woe. His shining maid is transformed into a "weeping Woman," as the translucent cabinet is burst asunder:

> I strove to seize the inmost form
> With ardour fierce and hands of flame,
> But burst the Crystal Cabinet,
> And like a weeping Babe became—
> A weeping Babe upon the wild,
> And weeping Woman pale reclin'd,
> And in the outward air again
> I fill'd with woes the passing wind.

This "ardour fierce" which for Keats would induce the highest
creativity and the highest value is for Blake an anathema,
destructive of pure delight. It is destructive for Blake because
the dancer has had a failure of vision. Caught up by the maiden
from his merry dance and locked within her gold and crystal
cabinet, the dancer cannot rejoice in his gold and crystal vision
of maid and England within. He demands more. Because he
cannot see with his spiritual eye, he struggles for a Wordsworthian truth which he can seize, instead of struggling for
clarity of his own vision. His imagination has only to grasp the
relationship between inner and outer, the inner truth and the
outer body, to recognize that the maid's "inmost form" is synonymous with her corporeal form. He lacks the Blakean vision,
apparent in a child in *The Chimney Sweeper* who can induce
warmth and happiness by his recognition that "when your
head's bare / You know that the soot cannot spoil your white
hair."

In a sense, the singer in Keats's *Ode to a Nightingale* is
tempted by the same transcendance as Wordsworth and Blake's
dancer. But Keats's singer welcomes his being tolled back to
sole self. Wisely, though sadly, he recognizes that complete
transcendence demands complete annihilation of self, denying
the very sensation that makes possible the imaginative leap.
Negative capability has made possible the leap; but a fear of
having ears in vain, becoming a sod to the high requiem of the
bird, demands a tolled return.

True, in *Lamia* the protagonist reveals no wisdom similar to
that experienced by the singer of the *Ode to a Nightingale*. On
the contrary, the ardor of Lycius' pursuit of the serpent-woman
is mitigated consistently by his lack of negative capability.
LAMIA, *II, 234–8* Although his imagination would follow an angel, his conceptual brain would clip its wings. Prompted by the sage Apollonius, his dull thoughts would unweave the rainbow, master all
mysteries, "empty the haunted air." The "sophist's eye" would
LAMIA, *II, 299–300* pierce all lovely dreams, "like a sharp spear." Under the dissecting vision of Apollonius, Lycius cannot be content with Adam's
dream. His solitary thinkings cannot dodge conception, leaving
the naked brain at the very bourn of heaven. Instead, like
Wordsworth, he feels impelled to reach irritably after truths.

And yet, in the earlier contrasting scene with Hermes and the
serpent, no such discontent with the life of sensations is evident.
Because "celestial heat / Burnt from his winged heels to either    LAMIA, *I, 22–3*
ear," Hermes swears his oath that he will transform the serpent
back to her woman's form, if only his ethereal vision of the
nymph becomes a reality. And Lamia, too, intent upon her own
pursuit of the youth in Corinth, makes possible the metamor-
phosis from "gordian shape of dazzling hue" to "lady bright."    LAMIA, *I, 47, 171*
Both Hermes and the serpent-woman succeed in their pursuit
of the life of sensations. Because they each possess negative
capability enormously, they can make real their waking dreams
through the intensity of the imaginative pursuit. Like Adam,
both awaken to find their dreams are true.

But for Lycius, under tutelage of a "trusty guide / And    LAMIA, *I, 375–6*
good instructor," Adam's dream is not enough. Without nega-
tive capability, his dreams can only shadow his own soul's    TO J. H. REYNOLDS,
daytime in the dark void of the night. In summer skies, he is    *70–1, 84*
forced to mourn. Even as he lies entwined within the rainbow,
only half intent upon ensnaring and trammeling up her soul in
his, he must reach irritably after speculative truths:

> Deafening the swallow's twitter, came a thrill    LAMIA, *II, 27–33*
> Of trumpets—Lycius started—the sounds fled,
> But left a thought a-buzzing in his head.
> For the first time, since first he harbour'd in
> That purple-lined palace of sweet sin,
> His spirit pass'd beyond its golden bourn
> Into the noisy world almost forsworn.

With that first thought, love is doomed, for "but a moment's    LAMIA, *II, 39*
thought is passion's passing bell," tolling him back to sole self.
At the "touch of cold philosophy," all charms fly. For the poet,    LAMIA, *II, 229–30*
as for all mortals who would create reality and worth, there
must first be a contentment in any "secret essence," the negative
capability which would make him see where learning has no
light.

Thus, when Keats writes in his "vale of Soul-making" letter
of the necessity for schooling an intelligence and making it a
soul, effecting an interaction between mind and heart in ele-

mental space, he would divert the mind from its search for intellectual truths and philosophical lights which lie outside human time dimensions. Where the heart must feel and suffer in a thousand diverse ways, the mind must rest content with secret essences and the half-truths available in the life of sensation. Not the cold light of truth, but the blazing torch of the heart illuminates the road which the soul must take. The mind must suck its identity through the teat of the heart; intelligence must be schooled by using the heart as its hornbook. If "the yearning Passion I have for the beautiful [is] connected and made one with the ambition of my intellect," then intellect must modify its aims, curbing its desires, resigning itself to half-knowledge, to doubts and mysteries. Rather than irritably reaching after fact and reason, it must learn to develop "negative capability."

Like the maker of souls, the creator of poetry must school the intelligence to follow the innate, the instinctive, the sensorial. The guiding hand of the mortal creator must rest upon the rudder of the imagination, not upon the charts and maps of abstract thinking. Far from smoothing the path for poetry, laws and precepts are dangerous rocks which threaten to dash our dreams to nothingness during our mortal storms. But to stay upon the green shore, play a silly pipe, take tea and comfortable advice from those who know the rocks is equally treacherous. To find salvation, one must leap for one's self into the sea —as Keats admits doing with *Endymion*—learning for one's self the soundings, the quicksands and the rocks. "The Genius of Poetry must work out its own salvation in a man: It cannot be matured by law & precept, but by sensation & watchfulness in itself—That which is creative must create itself."

*Ltr. to Hessey,*
*8 Oct. 1818*

Whoever pursues beauty must follow, not principles, but love and fellow-feeling. He must be content with

SLEEP AND POETRY,
*317–45*

> brotherhood,
> And friendliness the nurse of mutual good.
> The friendly grasp that sends a pleasant sonnet
> Into the brain ere one can think upon it;
> The silence when some rhymes are coming out;
> And when they're come, the very pleasant rout:
> The message certain to be done to-morrow . . .

Not conception, but the stir of a swan's neck, invisible amid the rushes, a butterfly nestling a rose, a linnet among the bushes—"Things such as these are ever harbingers / To trains of peaceful images."

Lacking an interaction with heart, mind alone is creative only of contrivance and artifice. Without the life of sensations, the pseudo-poet is productive only of false beauty, like those handicraftsmen of a prior age who thought they straddled Pegasus in their pursuit of reason. These are the men, nurtured alike by "foppery and barbarism," whom Keats addresses in *Sleep and Poetry:*

> The winds of heaven blew, the ocean roll'd
> Its gathering waves—ye felt it not. The blue
> Bared its eternal bosom, and the dew
> Of summer nights collected still to make
> The morning precious: beauty was awake!
> Why were ye not awake? But ye were dead
> To things ye knew not of,—were closely wed
> To musty laws lined out with wretched rule
> And compass vile: so that ye taught a school
> Of dolts to smooth, inlay, and clip, and fit,
> Till, like the certain wands of Jacob's wit,
> Their verses tallied.

SLEEP AND POETRY, *188–99*

The abandonment of *Hyperion* is coincident with Keats's recognition that "Miltonic verse cannot be written but in an artful or rather artist's humour." Despite his own attempts at producing "the true voice of feeling," too much of the Miltonic has resulted in "false beauty proceeding from art." To George and Georgiana, he confides, "I have but lately stood on my guard against Milton. Life to him would be death to me. Miltonic verse cannot be written but in the vein of art—I wish to devote myself to another sensation—." For Keats, the failure of *Hyperion* clearly marked a violation of his own "resolution, never to write for the sake of writing, or making a poem," never from contrivance or artfulness. The true poet cannot be too different from the thrush whose "song comes native with the warmth," even though it is itself lacking in knowledge. The creator of verse, like the creator of souls, weds himself, not to

*Ltr. to Reynolds, 21 Sept. 1819*

*Ltr. to George & Georgiana, 21 Sept. 1819*

*Ltr. to Haydon, 8 Mar. 1819*

O THOU WHOSE FACE

TO HOPE, *28*   compass and rule, but "to sigh out sonnets to the midnight air!"
Always, there must be awareness that

TO J. H. REYNOLDS,
*78–82*

> Imagination brought
> Beyond its proper bound, yet still confined,—
> Lost in a sort of Purgatory blind,
> Cannot refer to any standard law
> Of either earth or heaven.

*Ltr. to Hessey,*
*8 Oct. 1818*

*Ltr. to Reynolds,*
*9 Apr. 1818*

*Ltr. to Woodhouse,*
*27 Oct. 1818*

Not laws and precepts, but "love of beauty in the abstract"
should offer the sole motivating force behind creativity. "I have
not the slightest feel of humility towards the Public—or to
any thing in existence,—but the eternal Being, the Principle of
Beauty,—and the Memory of great Men," he confides to Reynolds. Even if he knew that all he wrote one night were to be
burned on the following morning, he is still assured that he
would "write from the mere yearning and fondness I have for
the Beautiful."

*Ltr. to George &*
*Tom,*
*21 Dec. 1817*

WHAT CAN I
DO, *14*

Nothing should detract the creator from his pursuit of Beauty
—not fame, not truth, no irritable reaching after fact and
reason, for "the excellence of every Art is its intensity, capable
of making all disagreeables evaporate, from their being in close
relationship with Beauty & [its] Truth." Capable of remaining
in a state of mystery, uncertainty, doubt, the great poet is one
who has developed negative capability. With him, "the sense
of Beauty overcomes every other consideration, or rather oblit-
erates all consideration." For him, as for Keats, though the
winged muse is "unintellectual, yet [it is] divine to me."

# 11
# Creative Technique:
# Perception as Knowledge

In the interaction of mind and heart within the world of elemental space, the ardent pursuit of the mortal creator must be innate, instinctive, sensorial. Although mind alone ought not to dominate the pursuit, neither should heart alone. Thought is not fully denigrated; the life of sensations has not displaced craft or knowledge. Certainly Garrod's edition of Keats's poetry, revealing the multiple variants that went into the making of some of the final versions, is itself indicative of the very conscious craftsmanship in which Keats was apparently engaged. But craft need not be identified with shackling laws, and mind is not always to be identified with dissecting analysis or restraining precepts.

In reviewing his efforts with *Endymion,* Keats laments that he has "written independently *without Judgment,*" and promises that hereafter he "may write independently & *with Judgment.*" A year later, he confides to Reynolds of his efforts with *Lamia* and *Otho the Great,* his "great hopes of success, because I make use of my Judgment more deliberately than I yet have done." And in his commentary on *La Belle Dame* he stresses the same need: "We must temper the Imagination as the Critics say with Judgment."

*Ltr. to Hessey,
8 Oct. 1818*

*Ltr. to Reynolds,
11 July 1819*

*Ltr. to George &
Georgiana,
21 Apr. 1819*

In the creative process, mind does not utterly succumb to heart, and thoughts do not give way totally to passions. On the contrary, mind or intelligence must maintain a limited but necessary capacity in judging, in affirmation or denial of the direction taken by the sympathetic imagination in moving the human heart toward its fullest identity. But "mind" for Keats is at its best meditative, not analytic. Perception is to be distinguished from conception. The mind must be the instrument of sympathy, of love, of embracive thought, not of isolating reason. It is a faculty of disinterested speculation or reflective judgment, not of dissecting, geometric cogitation:

*Ltr. to Reynolds,*
*3 May 1818*

An extensive knowledge is needful to thinking people—it takes away the heat and fever; and helps, by widening speculation, to ease the Burden of the Mystery. . . . The difference of high Sensations with and without knowledge appears to me this—in the latter case we are falling continually ten thousand fathoms deep and being blown up again without wings and with all [the] horror of a bare shouldered Creature—in the former case, our shoulders are fledge, and we go thro' the same air and space without fear.

*Ltr. to Bailey,*
*22 Nov. 1817*

In his letter to Bailey about Adam's dream, Keats had written: "O for a Life of Sensations rather than of Thoughts!" But as the poet himself well recognized, sensations without knowledge are anarchical: they lead only to chaos. At the mercy of every passing passion, we are buffeted about like leaves driven by the west wind: helpless, unprotected, expugnable, open to every danger. Thought without sensation is tyrannical: it leads only to subjection and enslavement. To move through the world of elemental space without fear, to ease away the fever and the fret, we must grow wings to seek our immortality. Mind and heart must interact to sprout a soul. Emulating the sweet sonnet, fettered in spite of loveliness, we must wreathe a flowery band to bind us to the earth—in spite of despondence or the dearth of noble natures:

IF BY DULL RHYMES

If by dull rhymes our English must be chain'd,
And, like Andromeda, the Sonnet sweet
Fetter'd, in spite of pained loveliness;
Let us find out, if we must be constrain'd,

Sandals more interwoven and complete
To fit the naked foot of poesy:
Let us inspect the lyre, and weigh the stress
Of every chord, and see what may be gain'd
By ear industrious, and attention meet;
Misers of sound and syllable, no less
Than Midas of his coinage, let us be
Jealous of dead leaves in the bay wreath crown;
So, if we may not let the Muse be free,
She will be bound with garlands of her own.

Indicative of his concern with poetic craftsmanship, this sonnet on the sonnet is included in a letter where Keats writes of his endeavor "to discover a better Sonnet Stanza than we have. The legitimate does not suit the language over-well from the pouncing rhymes—the other kind appears too elegiac—and the couplet at the end of it has seldom a pleasing effect." Keats then transcribes several sonnets and the *Ode to Psyche,* apparently indicative of the poet's attempts "to discover a better Sonnet Stanza."

*Ltr. to George & Georgiana, 30 Apr. 1819*

The distinction Keats raises here between the legitimate or Petrarchan sonnet and the Shakespearean is typical of his day. When the sonnet was revived by mid-eighteenth century, following its decline after Milton, sonneteers turned mainly to their own irregular inventions or to Petrarch and the Italian strain for guidance. They turned to Petrarch, not because he offered a perfection of the form—as Virgil had offered the preceding age a perfection of the epic—but rather because he had invented the sonnet and could reveal within it his own originality and his imaginative genius. In his *Conjectures on Original Composition,* Edward Young had differentiated between originals and imitations: *"Originals* are the fairest flowers: *Imitations* are of quicker growth, but fainter bloom." Distinct from the ancients who could not be imitators, moderns "have a merit in their power. They may soar in the regions of *liberty,* or move in the soft fetters of easy *imitation.* . . ." Even in this mid-eighteenth-century treatise, the terms of Keats's letter on the sonnet are clear: the Petrarchan sonnet is "legitimate," because it is original and natural, while the Shakespear-

ean sonnet, a copy or imitation of the pre-existent form, is "illegitimate" or unnatural.

When Keats undertakes "to discover a better Sonnet Stanza than we have," he would liberate the form from the fetters superimposed by the "illegitimate" sonneteers, like Shakespeare and Milton. To improve upon the form, Keats gives rise within the sonnet to three exhortations: first, "Let us find . . . sandals . . . to fit the naked foot of poesy"; second, inspecting the lyre and weighing each stress, "Let us . . . see what may be gain'd by ear industrious, and attention meet"; and third, "let us be jealous of dead leaves in the bay wreath crown." But these three exhortations are contingent upon an assumption, couched in three conditional clauses: that "our English must be chain'd, and . . . fetter'd"; that "we must be constrain'd"; and that "we may not let the Muse be free."

Thus, the assumed conditions of restraint are all countered by Keats with three exhortations, that we pay some attention to craft. But craft or *techné* here, as elsewhere in Keats, has no referent to conceptual knowledge, to a world of pre-existent forms so implicit in Plato's *Ion*. Nor is it Keats's intent to create "Nature to advantage dress'd," as Pope suggests in his *Essay on Criticism,* where an advantageous dressing of nature is dependent upon a knowledge of the world as it once was, out of the hands of a perfect Creator. To bind the muse "with garlands of her own" is to provide a dress most befitting her natural, pristine state. Like the flowery band in Endymion which should "bind us to the earth," the Muse's "bay wreath crown" ought to provide an appropriate fetter for this "painted loveliness," this thing of beauty within the bitter-sweet world.

Clearly, it is not craft, not *techné*, that Keats is objecting to in his endeavor "to discover a better sonnet stanza"; it is not knowledge or a poetic consciousness. What he objects to is an art which has become artifice, a knowledge encumbered by *a priori* precepts, a consciousness dictated by intellectual laws.

Sir Philip Sidney suggests that the final end of the poet is "to lift up the mind from the dungeon of the body, to the enjoying of his owne divine essence." And Samuel Daniel announces in his *Defence of Ryme* that the constriction of the sonnet form, "being farre more laborious than loose measures . . . must

needs, meeting with wit and industry, breed greater and worthier effects in our language." For Daniel the tight constriction of rhymed verse offers a challenge. It gives the poet "wings to mount and carries him, not out of his course, but as it were beyond his power to a farre happier flight." Daniel offers a typical Renaissance appraisal:

Al excellencies being sold us at the hard price of labour, it followes, where we bestow most thereof, we buy the best successe. . . . So that if our labours have wrought out a manumission from bondage, and that wee goe at libertie, notwithstanding these ties, wee are no longer the slaves of Ryme, but we make it a most excellent instrument to serve us.

For the Renaissance poet, verse form—especially the restricted fourteen-line sonnet form—offers this kind of "dungeon." We are in "bondage" to it, and it threatens to make us "slaves." It shackles; it imprisons; it enchains. But with ingenuity and industry, with wit and invention, with craft and knowledge of techniques, the sonneteer with a master hand can rise above the restrictions to enjoy "his owne divine essence." He can become like unto a "second-deity." As Montaigne had observed in *Of Experience,* man finds "greatness of soul is not so much pressing upward and forward as knowing how to set oneself in order and circumscribe oneself." By setting himself in order, by seeing with clarity his own limitations within the shackling form, the sonneteer can develop the potential for his own greatness. In his final chapter of *The Prince,* Machiavelli had viewed the relationship between bondage and greatness of soul in an analogous way:

. . . It was necessary in order to make apparent the virtue of Moses, that the people of Israel should be enslaved in Egypt, and that the Persians should be oppressed by the Medes to provide an opportunity to illustrate the greatness and the spirit of Cyrus, and that the Athenians should be scattered in order to show the excellence of Theseus, thus at the present time, in order to reveal the valor of an Italian spirit it was essential that Italy should fall to her present low estate, more enslaved than the Hebrews, more servile than the Persians, more disunited than the Athenians, leaderless and lawless, beaten, despoiled, lacerated, overrun and crushed under every kind of misfortune.

But the romantic soul sees no challenge in restrictions. It wants the wings to mount, but without the laboriousness of earthbound measures. It wants greatness of soul, but without circumscription. Gravitating toward perfection, it wants no reminder of our degenerate soul. Shackles of every kind are distasteful impediments. In the name of liberty, Shelley frees Prometheus. Blake laments in *Songs of Experience:*

> In every cry of every Man,
> In every Infant's cry of fear,
> In every voice, in every ban,
> The mind-forg'd manacles I hear.

At the opening of *The Social Contract,* Rousseau observes that "Man is born free; and everywhere he is in chains." Marx and Engels conclude their *Manifesto* with a cry for the unity of workingmen: "The proletarians have nothing to lose but their chains. They have a world to win."

Restrictive laws, which for the Renaissance offer a challenge to test nobility and greatness, are for Keats and the romantics the abode of the Sirens. Like Odysseus, who stuffed with wax the ears of his companions in order that they might not be lured by these songs to death and destruction, the Keatsian poet in search of true creativity must turn a deaf ear to those illegitimate songs prompted by shackling intellect, songs which would dash our dreams to nothingness.

Our identity, our immortality, our poetry, our soul, cannot be achieved by prior restrictions which challenge us to lift our degenerate souls from these clayey lodgings. This can be achieved, if we are to follow Keats's advice, only by a proper interaction of heart and mind, the sweet and the bitter, the pleasure and the pain, by finding

> Sandals more interwoven and complete
> To fit the naked foot of poesy.

Not constriction, but a butterfly nestling a rose with all its thorns, the hearty grasp of fellow-feeling amid the burning fever and the parching tongue—these are the harbingers of

poetry. Thus, Keats is convinced that "the only means of strengthening one's intellect is to make up ones mind about nothing—to let the mind be a thoroughfare for all thoughts. Not a select party." Intellectually, one resolves upon nothing.

*Ltr. to George & Georgiana, 24 Sept. 1819*

Like axioms in philosophy, axioms in poetry "are not axioms until they are proved upon our pulses: We read fine—things but never feel them to the full until we have gone the same steps as the Author." Our own imagination must be persuaded to strain for the light of beauty in the midst of the penetralium of mystery and doubt. Penetrated only through the intensity of an ardent pursuit, beauty holds forth its truth—insufficient for the ratiocinative man, but enough for the man of sensations —that it can deliver us from "the weariness, the fever, and the fret."

*Ltr. to Reynolds, 3 May 1818*

# The Keatsian
# Aftermath

I asked no help of books,
for I believed that the truth
I sought would come to me
like the subject of a poem,
from some moment
of passionate experience. . . .
—William Butler Yeats,
*The Trembling of the Veil* (III, 7).

# 12
# Joyce, Freud, and the Internalization of Order

In his early verse, Keats had written of the "liberty" that might be gleaned from a vast idea rolling ever before him, about the aim and end of poetry: that "it should be a friend / To soothe the cares, and lift the thoughts of man." SLEEP AND POETRY, *245–7, 290–304*

> Therefore should I
> Be but the essence of deformity,
> A coward, did my very eye-lids wink
> At speaking out what I have dared to think.
> Ah! rather let me like a madman run
> Over some precipice; let the hot sun
> Melt my Dedalian wings, and drive me down
> Convuls'd and headlong!

This image of the poet as a winged creature has long been a commonplace in the history of poetry and poetic theory. Even Socrates in the *Ion* had alluded to the poet as "a light and winged and sacred thing," a subtle mutation of Pegasus, the winged horse of the Muses. The image has had an understandable appeal to nineteenth-century sensibilities. In these particular lines by Keats, the delicate blending of Pegasus with Deda-

lus somewhat redeems the image from the sentimental clichés
of romanticism.

In Ovid and Apollodorus, as in the whole of Greek and
Roman mythology, Dedalus appears as a master craftsman. He
is an ingenious artificer and inventor, instructed in his craft,
according to some sources, by Pallas Athene herself. In his
escape from Crete, Dedalus made two sets of wings, binding
together the feathers by means of wax—one set for himself, the
second for his son Icarus. With Dedalus, a knowledge of craft,
accompanied by wisdom in the use of the wings, led ultimately
to liberty; but Icarus, heedless of the parental warning not to
soar too high lest the wax be melted by the heat of the sun,
plunges to his death into the seas.

In these lines from *Sleep and Poetry*, the poetic flight is not
identified with Dedalian artifice and cunning. Here, as elsewhere in Keats, the poetic flight is associated with the chariot of
the imagination, with ardent flights and dizzied ascents. But
then the Keatsian flight with "Dedalian wings" is not to be
identified with the ignorance and naiveté of Icarus, the madness and death, the *amabilis insania* sometimes identified with
creativity. Keats is quite specific about alternatives. Unless the
creative artist has the freedom of "speaking out what I have
dared to think," breaking the fetters which would hold back
the dizzied flight of the creative imagination, then Keats would
drive himself "like a madman" down some precipice, "con-
vuls'd and headlong." Madness is here the alternative to liberty; death, to creativity. The wings can be used in the service of
freedom and creativity—but they can also be misused, for madness and for death.

Much of what Keats envisions for the poet's "Dedalian
wings" in *Sleep and Poetry* is at work with Stephen Dedalus in
Joyce's *A Portrait of the Artist as a Young Man*. Like Keats, the
hero of Joyce's novel is developing an aesthetic, one which
would allow for the freeing of his own artistic fetters. For
Stephen, freedom is concomitant with knowledge; the creation
of beauty, closely allied to a measure of truth. But in Joyce's
novel, liberty and beauty are to be identified with self-percep-
tion and self-knowledge—not with the ardent interaction of self

and object as with Keats, or with a set of cosmic absolutes as with Keats's predecessors.

The principles of Stephen's aesthetic emerge at the close of Joyce's novel, simultaneous with his decision to leave Ireland. Although the two pronouncements—the departure and principles—are presented independently, it is relatively clear within the context of the final chapter that they are interdependent and illustrative of the single act. The creation of beauty is for Stephen dependent upon separation from Ireland; divorce from Ireland is predicated upon intentions to be creative of beauty. If his commitment to art is to be realized, the claims of family, church, nation must be subjected to intellectual scrutiny. They must be analyzed, coldly and objectively. Their various and conflicting demands must be broken down. "When the soul of a man is born in this country, there are nets flung at it to hold it back from flight . . . nationality, language, religion. I shall try to fly by those nets," announces the twentieth-century Dedalus. To forge ahead to a disentangled future, where true creativity is possible, the artist must free himself from the imprisoning demands of the past. From the prison gates of his soul, he must create his own integrity: a wholeness, a symmetry, a radiance.

Like Endymion who through ardent love would have "escap'd from dull mortality's harsh net," Joyce's young artist must "disentangle the subtle soul of the image from its mesh of defining circumstances most exactly and 're-embody' it in artistic circumstances chosen as the most exact for it in its new office." Gifted with twin faculties, the selective and the reproductive, the Joycean artist is free to select and to reproduce only when he has evaded those nets which would capture his soul and fling it earthward. Unlike Keats who would wreathe the flowery band to bind us to the earth, binding the fettered Muse with garlands of her own, Stephen as artist must anticipate a disentangled future, free of circumscription. Only then can he apprehend *integritas,* the wholeness of a thing; *consonantia,* its true complexity and harmony; *claritas,* its ultimate radiance, the luminous silent stasis of aesthetic pleasure which would enchant the heart. Like Dedalus the hawkman, the true crafts-

ENDYMION,
*III, 907*

man must be boundless with his wings of wax, hurtling toward
the sun over the sea.

Stephen himself looks upon his theory as an extension and
clarification of Aquinas. Yet the psychology is more Freudian
than Thomistic, more twentieth-century than medieval. His
ethics have more in common with *The Psychopathology of
Everyday Life* than with the *Summa Theologica*. And his artistry shares in the world of forms developed in the novel by
Henry James and Marcel Proust, in painting by Picasso and
Dali, in sculpture by Henry Moore and Jacques Lipschitz, in
architecture by Frank Lloyd Wright and Le Corbusier. These
artistic forms are remote from Dante's structure in *The Divine
Comedy* or in the rebuilding of St.-Denis by Abbot Suger, but
not too removed from the structure of *Ode on a Grecian Urn*.
For Stephen, fulfillment in art is predicated upon his ability to
attain psychological freedom, to avoid the pitfalls of infantile
repressions and adolescent fears, the distorted conscience of
home and church and nation which would impinge upon the
young artist's powers of selection and reproduction. Only he
who achieves a whole and harmonious self can achieve wholeness and harmony in art. Success in art is wholly dependent
upon the freedom of the ego to control the approaches to
motility: the consuming demands of the id, the restricting
forces of the superego, the engulfing claims of the external
world.

As a prototype for the stream-of-consciousness novel, *A Portrait of the Artist as a Young Man* seems to offer a representation of an ordering which is wholly internal. Even the aesthetic
theory emerging in the final chapter is part of the larger whole
which is Stephen, a development from the songs and smells and
stories which confront the "nicens little boy named baby tuc-
koo" at the opening of the text. From the single consciousness
filter reality and worth. As long as the external world is subordinated to the internal consciousness and absorbed within it,
values are relative to this inner being. Significances are personal, individual, and highly relative. Internal chronology is
the only meaningful time-dimension, and art which captures
inner time is simply the vision of the world from the standpoint
of an individual constituted after a particular fashion. Because

humanity is immense, reality must have myriad forms. From the Joycean perspective, the reality of Stephen Dedalus and that of Endymion are not necessarily models. They are only representations of reality as perceived by two distinctly different creators.

Joyce's novel is, of course, no psychological case study of Stephen Dedalus, built upon Freudian principles. It is a work of art—just as Keats, interacting with Adam Smith's theory of the sympathetic imagination, produces the artistry of the *Ode on a Grecian Urn;* as Shakespeare, assuming the psychology of humors, creates *Hamlet;* and as Zola, operating upon principles of biological determinism, creates *Nana* and *Germinal.* What differentiates *Hamlet* from Burton's *Anatomy of Melancholy, Germinal* from Darwin's *The Descent of Man,* and Keats's verse from *The Theory of Moral Sentiments* is the selection and arrangement of materials for a given artistic end. Burton, Smith, and Darwin all arrange their work to fulfill didactic purposes. The results may indeed be art, although they are not writing poetry or drama or novels.

Two distinctly different kinds of form are perceptible in all these works. There is the artistic form—of narrative poetry or prose, which Keats shares with Shakespeare and Zola; and of persuasive prose, which Adam Smith shares with Burton and Darwin. But there is also a cultural form, a way of ordering attitudes and ideas. This is a form which Keats shares more with Adam Smith than with Zola or Shakespeare. The artistic may reflect the cultural: what Shakespeare does with the sonnet is somewhat dictated by his "Renaissance" way of looking upon experience. What Keats does with the sonnet is, in the same way, colored by his early nineteenth-century attitudes.

For Joyce, the mimetic act suggests an ordering which is individual and internal. Joyce's aesthetic in *Portrait* is not predicated upon the existence of an objective and external order toward which the art corresponds, like a microcosm of Shakespeare's and Burton's larger universe. Nor does it assume a Keatsian separation of subject and object, where self must be hurled into an ardent interaction with the non-self, trusting to the intensity of the experience to provide a coupling of two alienated forms. On the contrary, objects and events in young

Stephen's life seem to have no reality and no worth outside of his own consciousness. Language, nation, church, home have all impinged upon him and gone into his making. Yet they have not determined the structure of his being, any more than they have determined the structure of his novel or of his aesthetic theory. As long as their claims can be scrutinized and broken down, their influences rejected, their order abandoned, a new order of things can conceivably emerge. The mesh of defining circumstances, we are assured by Stephen, can be disentangled from the subtle soul of the image. The true muse, seemingly, will admit no fettering, except of the artist's own and deliberate making. The nets can be evaded. Indeed, if craft is to be based upon principles of free selection and free reproduction, rather than upon principles of personal pleasure and private pain, then the nets must be evaded.

Earlier, our point of departure was Plato's *Ion,* where Socrates drew the now familiar distinction between an art founded upon reason and knowledge and that which resulted from inspiration. Like all men, the artist must base his life, as well as his art, upon those rational principles which propel men toward the best. Thus, Socrates can in the *Phaedrus* liken the nature of a soul to a charioteer with a pair of winged horses: one of noble breed, upright, white, a lover of honor and glory; the other, ignoble and of ignoble breed, of a dark color, crooked and lumbering, a mate of insolence and pride, scarcely yielding to whip and spur. The happiness of the charioteer is of course dependent upon his control of these horses. He must develop a craft, a *techné,* which would bring peace to these disharmonious steeds that would tear each man in two. If he masters the two, enslaving the vicious and emancipating the virtuous, he will lead an orderly and harmonious, and hence a happy life.

But the master of Stephen Dedalus' riding academy is less Socrates than Freud, for whom horsemanship is a matter of psychology rather than ethics. The equestrian in Freud must manage not two but three unruly jades. He aims at the development of a *media via* still, but through an ego sufficiently strong and sufficiently free to bend the horses to his own will. Somehow, he must manage to reconcile the divergent claims of three

harsh tyrants: the external world, the superego, and the id. More important, the white steed described by Socrates assumes its reality, as well as its significance, from a pre-existent world of pure forms, one which for Socrates exists with absoluteness. The Socratic charioteer is informed of his craft, his control of the horses, by this very real world of values. But the Freudian horseman must learn that the value of his external world is highly dependent upon and likely to emerge from the subjective and personal world that lies within. In its relationship to the id, the ego must substitute a reality principle for a pleasure principle. Reason and sanity must replace the passions, and perception must displace instinct. We may long for absolute truths, even while recognizing their relativism. We may strive for a permanence of form within the world of calendrical time and bound by the poles of birth and death, but we must recognize that the stability of the ego within a world of individual, psychological time offers the only permanence we can inherit.

The Joycean structure offers an understandable development of directions taken by Keats and his contemporaries who had rejected the *a priori* existence of absolutes so basic to the early eighteenth-century world and the tradition which it inherited. Keatsian values, neither wholly external nor internal, arise from a perpetual interchange between the world within and the world without. In the flash and counter-flash of meeting reside all significances. Knowledge emerges from this experiential world, just as values and art arise from the steady encroachment of self upon the world of things.

In the final analysis, Joyce's novel and the aesthetic theory inextricably bound up with its structure are not the basis for impressionism—consonant with the music of Debussy and Ravel, or the paintings of Manet and Cézanne. Nor are they the basis for naturalism, paralleling the mechanism of Zola's and Dreiser's novels, the paintings of Léger and Piet Mondrian, and the cubistic drawings of Picasso and Braque. Both impressionism and naturalism are dependent upon nineteenth-century assumptions about a separation of subject and object. Yet impressionism lacks the clarity and rigid analysis to which Stephen's warring impressions give way before the close of

Joyce's novel; and naturalism never provides an alternative, as Joyce obviously does, to the mechanics of cause-and-effect relationships. Stephen emerges, not as the victim of his warring impressions, but potentially as their master. Dedalus, the modern craftsman, acquires a knowledge, a *techné*, that is to direct his craft. Ultimately, knowledge for Stephen is not based upon a private apprehension of multiple sensations. But then it does not rest upon an *a priori* world of Platonic forms, the cosmic harmonies of Shakespeare, or the mechanical concatenations of Zola's materialistic and deterministic universe. Having evaded the nets of home and family, church and nation, Stephen is on the way to becoming master of his own soul. His self-knowledge can open the way to freedom, and from this freedom can emerge true creativity. Almost like the "second-deity" of the Renaissance, he can with sufficient strength and maturity bring into being a whole new world—perhaps not the chimeras and cylops that Sir Philip Sidney speaks of in his *Apologie;* but certainly the world of *Araby* and *The Dead,* the sirens in *Ulysses,* and the vast panorama of *Finnegan's Wake.*

Because the Renaissance artist could assume the existence of a First and Efficient Cause who had put both man and an independent nature into being, he was himself provided with organizing principles for his own mimetic act. By his craft, his knowledge of pre-existent forms, the second-deity could offer a representation modeled after the divine harmonies of the universe. He might, as Sidney had suggested, make things "either better than Nature bringeth forth, or quite newe formes," for the artist was not limited by the gifts of nature. He was "not inclosed within the narrow warrant of her guifts, but freely ranging onely within the Zodiack of his owne wit." But in improving upon nature or adding to its forms, the new deity strove—as nature herself was incapable—toward a correspondence with universal harmony, as revealed to "the Zodiack of his owne wit." Since his wit and inventiveness were themselves a creation of his Maker, the free range of "his owne wit" gave "right honor to the heavenly Maker of that maker; who having made man to his owne likenes, set him beyond and over all the workes of that seconde nature. . . ." Thus, from the Renaissance perspective, the fleshiness of Botticelli's creations, the

muscular sculpture of Michelangelo, the sensuous verse of Marlowe's *Hero and Leander,* the balanced prose of Lyly's *Endymion* are not projected as a mirrored representation of what is already within nature. They are either improvements upon nature or new forms, new harmonies, new orders, none of which is to be found within nature—though they may indeed exist within the larger harmony of their Divine Creator who is set off from nature.

But assumptions about a harmonious universe and an efficient First Cause, so central to the Renaissance concept of the second deity, are rarely at work in the early nineteenth-century artist. Without a theological core, Keats's second deity cannot structure the multiplicity and variety within nature, improving it to correspond with divine order. Nor in the creation of totally new forms can his craft be guided by a knowledge of any external order. Indeed, it took the major part of his century to discern that, if ordering principles cannot come from without, they may come from within. Although they cannot be derived rationally, they may be derived experientially. They may no longer emerge from a symmetrical and harmonious deity; still, they can conceivably emerge from the "second-deity" himself.

"Every mental pursuit takes its reality and worth from the *Ltr. to Bailey,* ardour of the pursuer," Keats had written to Bailey. The world *13 Mar. 1818* of things can itself be made "Great and dignified by an ardent pursuit." The more ardent the pursuit and the more intensive the interaction between pursuer and pursued, the more reality and worth to be attributed to both. For Keats, of course, reality and worth are not to be discerned in the substance or in the order of external things, really or ideally; nor are they to be found wholly in the internal world of sensation, impression, or feeling. The Keatsian creative process is dependent for its structure both upon the things of beauty that are forever a joy and upon him who wreathes of them a flowery band to bind him to the earth. It demands a human interaction between man and nightingales, man and urns, man and crickets, man and other men. It emerges from the hierarchical transition between the individual sensual experience taking place within the world of calendrical time and the subtle merging that can occur only

within the imaginative, personalized, dream-like world of eternality. It hovers between and among the multiple contents of the earth and the gradual formation of a soul, as self fades and dissolves into these contents.

This is, with Keats, not yet the complete absorption and annihilation of externality, such as we are to encounter in the twentieth century with Kafka and Proust, Miro and Dali, where the reality and worth of men and things are wholly relative to the individual's vision. By the twentieth century, each man can become a potential "second-deity," and the individual psyche can become the only means of determining both existence and essence. For Keats, as well as his contemporaries, the primacy of fellow-feeling, brotherhood, social love, dominates the creative act and effectively structures the disparate elements that previously had derived their unity from godhead alone. But twentieth-century art and criticism are rarely social or collective. Like Stephen's vision, which does not demand for the artist's craft an impassioned social love, a fellow-feeling which for Keats could enable the sympathetic imagination to ensnare and trammel up one soul within another, twentieth-century values tend to be individual, isolated, personal, subjective, relative, and highly attenuated. Lacking a faith in external laws, we have turned increasingly to our only certitude—a knowledge of self.

# 13

# The Old World of Mr. Eliot
# and the New World of
# Mr. Brooks

If only because he was so articulate in his double role as poet and as critic, T. S. Eliot has emerged from the world of letters, perhaps more than anyone, as representative of the twentieth century. The distinction raised in his 1921 essay on Donne and the metaphysicals is by now a familiar one. Seventeenth-century poets possessed a mechanism of sensibility which could devour any kind of experience, said Mr. Eliot. But during the latter half of their century, under the influence of Milton and Dryden, a "dissociation of sensibility" set in, one from which we presumably never recovered. Under Gray and Collins, Johnson and Goldsmith, language may have become more refined, but feeling became more crude. In revolting against the ratiocinative and descriptive, poets of the sentimental age "thought and felt by fits, unbalanced; they reflected. In one or two passages of Shelley's *Triumph of Life,* in the second *Hyperion,* there are traces of a struggle toward unification of sensibility. But Keats and Shelley died, and Tennyson and Browning ruminated." Mr. Eliot concluded his justly famous and most influential essay with the reflection that Donne, Vaughan, Herbert, Crashaw were all "in the direct current of

English poetry," a current which somehow between Milton and Eliot himself had been deflected.

By 1947 Eliot was prepared to concede "that poets are [now] sufficiently removed from Milton, and sufficiently liberated from his reputation, to approach the study of his work without danger, and with profit to their poetry and to the English language." Further, "if such a dissociation did take place, I suspect that the causes are too complex and too profound to justify our accounting for the change in terms of literary criticism." By 1947 Keats and Milton, Tennyson, and even Rudyard Kipling had all been approached by Eliot—apparently "without danger, and with profit." But the *tradition* or *direct current* was still rather puzzling. The mainstream of English tradition clearly included both Keats and Donne, but if we were to approach either properly—"without danger, and with profit"—we still needed a knowledge of that "current." I myself would have found it difficult to exclude from that "current" two and a half centuries of English poetry. Eliot was for some time of the same mind, although his many imitators still tend to think in terms of a dissociation of thought and feeling in turning to the complexities of eighteenth- and nineteenth-century poetry in England.

Today, the enigma so often touted during the years that Eliot reigned as literary savant has been considerably clarified. For a long time the poetic revolution he had effected seemed incompatible with his conservative politics and religion. We see now, as we might have been incapable of seeing several decades ago, that the poetic revolution was radical only insofar as it offered a drastic and necessary shift, in poetic as well as in critical standards, away from the morass of Victorian clichés and sentimentality. Mr. Eliot wanted to clear the decks, get rid of the stagnant language, the clichés of emotion, the stereotyped thought which had evolved in the tradition since Donne and the metaphysicals. In those early days of the 1920's and 1930's, Eliot offered a clear-cut voice, assertive and at once convincing, insistent upon the reaffirmation of standards and values—in literary criticism no less than in the poetry emerging from the tradition. But we see now that there are revolutions and counter-revolutions—revolutions of the left, and of the

right. We see now that, hearkening back to the metaphysicals who were themselves extending implications of the Renaissance, Eliot was offering a reactionary poetic, at one with his politics and religion. We see now that poetic "unification of sensibility" was for Eliot coincident with political and theological unification: with Anglo-Catholicism and Royalism. *Prufrock* and *The Wasteland* and *Ash Wednesday*—like the essays on Shakespeare and Dante and Donne, the two essays on Milton, and the various essays on literature—have much in common with *Notes Toward the Definition of Culture* and *The Idea of a Christian Society*. As early as 1936, Eliot had written in *Religion and Culture* about this common ground: "In ages like our own, in which there is no . . . common agreement, it is the more necessary for Christian readers to scrutinize their reading, especially of works of imagination, with explicit ethical and theological standards." The essay on religion might well have served as a commentary on the Donne essay, for Mr. Eliot affirmed "that the whole of modern literature is corrupted by what I call Secularism, that it is simply unaware of, simply cannot understand the meaning of, the primacy of the supernatural over the natural life: of something which I assume to be our primary concern."

This kind of statement is, of course, most un-Keatsian. Indeed, it is anti-Keatsian, if we recognize that Keats's notion about soul-making and poetry-creation is directly aimed at deflecting the "supernatural" and the "theological" through the secular.

We see now that Eliot's poetic and critical standards were clearly dependent upon "ethical and theological standards"— standards explicit in the early seventeenth century in England, but more or less called into question since that time. Milton did his best to justify them; they were somewhat vindicated by Pope; the later Wordsworth and Matthew Arnold (early *and* late) tried to prop up the standards—but with decreasing success. By the late nineteenth century, these standards were no longer so "explicit." They had been challenged by Voltaire, Rousseau, Diderot and Darwin; by Mill, Comte, and Marx; by Keats and Shelley; by George Eliot and Conrad.

These were standards which Keats in his very secular "vale of

Soul-making" letter is intent upon discounting. "I do not at all believe in this sort of perfectibility . . . the world will not admit of it. . . . The point at which Man may arrive is as far as the parallel state in inanimate nature and no further," he was to write to George and Georgiana, offering "a grander system of salvation than the chrystain religion— . . . a system of Spirit-creation." The interaction of self and non-self in Keats, the experiential interaction of the experiencing *I* and the experienced *it,* is projected as the basis for the holiness of the heart's affection, the truth of Adam's dream. And this "corrupted . . . Secularism" is far removed from the "ethical and theological standards" explicit in Donne—and in T. S. Eliot himself.

If we trace the development of English poetry from Donne to T. S. Eliot, in pursuit of a very unified sensibility and very explicit standards, then Keats is indeed outside the "main current" of English poetry. But the tradition Eliot was talking about is the Christian tradition—and this, I would contend, is a singular limitation. I would have thought that a new view of tradition—somewhat less insular and exclusive—might have been introduced to England by the French *philosophes* at the close of the eighteenth century, or by the repeal of the Test and Corporation Act in 1828, by the Catholic Emancipation Bill of 1829, or by the Charles Bradlaugh case several decades later.

On the other hand, Keats is very much inside the "main current" if we turn for modern standards, not to Eliot, but to a theologian like Martin Buber who was to recognize, "That which will eventually play as an accustomed object around the man who is fully developed, must be wooed and won by the developing man in strenuous action." Almost in affirmation of the Keatsian process, Buber was to write in *I And Thou:*

For no *thing* is a ready-made part of an experience; only in the strength, acting and being acted upon, of what is over against men, is anything made accessible. Like primitive man the child lives between sleep and sleep (a great part of his waking hours is also sleep) in the flash and counter-flash of meeting.

The "main current" is equally perceptible in a scientist like Albert Einstein who could discern in the doctrine of a personal anthropomorphic deity the sublimation of a primitive concep-

tion of magic and prayer. This is a doctrine which, by virtue of its simplicity (according to Einstein), is accessible to the most undeveloped mind—but it ought not to become the refuge for the egocentric cravings of the teachers of science or of religion who ought, properly, to devote themselves to a far-reaching emancipation from the shackles of personal hopes and desires by way of the understanding. The same kind of observation might have been made about the teachers of poetry, the critics whose function it is to enhance our understanding of the art. From his scientist's perspective, Einstein is certainly enunciating a truth closely akin to Freud's apprehensions about the pleasure principle—in particular, implications drawn in *The Future of an Illusion,* and in that more controversial work, *Civilization and its Discontents,* about the need to master the derangements of communal life caused by the human instinct of aggression and self-destruction.

If we speak of *a* tradition or *the* tradition—one which presumably encompasses the poetic, rather than being distinct from it or subordinated to the theological or ethical—then Keats's *Ode to a Nightingale* would appear to lie more within that tradition than *Ash Wednesday* or the *Four Quartets.* Keats's letter to George and Georgiana about the "vale of Soul-making," to Woodhouse about the "poetical Character," to Bailey about Adam's dream seem more within that tradition than *The Metaphysical Poets,* the two *Milton* essays, or *The Idea of a Christian Society.* They seem more within that tradition, if only because they see with greater clarity how that tradition has emerged, and where it is heading—where, indeed, it must head.

Actually, Eliot is no less within that tradition—the tradition, not of Christian poetry, but of Western thought and culture—than Samuel Johnson or Byron, or Rudyard Kipling. But the tradition of English poetry, that poetry consonant with the mainstream of Western culture, takes us from Chaucer, Shakespeare, Donne, through Milton and Pope and Blake—to Keats —and to Hopkins, Hardy, the later Yeats, and Dylan Thomas. Mr. Eliot is without question within the tradition. How is it possible for anyone not to be within his own tradition? But it is absurd to consider him within the mainstream of that tradi-

tion. He is, rather, an anomaly—a powerful and effective anomaly—because he is a twentieth-century poet and critic, intent upon seventeenth-century poetics, politics, and religion. Like Shakespeare's Richard the Second, intent upon the pageantry of a medieval world, ceremonious before the pragmatic onslaught of a man of action, and dependent for his scepter, mace, and crown upon the powers of an omnipotent deity, Eliot has been grandiloquent, effusive, magnificent . . . but more out-of-date than the psychology of humors or yesterday's newspaper.

If we want a modern, a critic wholly within the twentieth century, we have only to turn to Cleanth Brooks or to the "new" critics who have followed in his footsteps. To some extent, Brooks's methods and principles derived from T. S. Eliot, with some immediate debts to I. A. Richards and to F. R. Leavis, among others. Brooks was very much aware of the tradition—and very sympathetic with it. But his view of history, particularly in his earlier writings, seemed somewhat restricted to those common paradoxical elements at work within history. Turning his attention to the literary works themselves, Brooks concentrated upon a close analysis of the language in which they were embodied. He and his followers were instrumental in placing an increasing emphasis upon the formal unity of a work of art. Like Eliot, Brooks was intent upon turning to the very language of poetry itself. Eliot wanted to counter the diffuse and dissociated language of his immediate predecessors, the poets whose language he was disavowing. Brooks's intent, that of a critic rather than a craftsman, was to disavow any distortion of poetry through the misleading language of criticism which might reduce the language of poetry to the language of statement through paraphrase; which might distort poetry through impressionism and subjectivism; which might offer biography or history or ethics or theology as a surrogate for the art; which might examine sources and analogues as the basis for critical analysis. Both men moved us in a necessary direction—Eliot with poetry, Brooks with criticism—into the structure of language itself. But for Eliot, the ultimate test of poetry or criticism lay in "explicit ethical and theological standards," distinct from a corrupted secularism. For

Brooks, whose antecedents were Poe and Henry James, criticism was to consider art only in relationship to its own form.

As a "simulacrum of reality," a poem must necessarily be taken "out of competition with scientific, historical, and philosophical propositions," said Mr. Brooks. Art must stand on its own—with its own tensions, its own paradoxes, its own complexities. In diverging from Eliot, Brooks voiced his suspicions about the terms *good* and *bad,* "meaningless terms when used absolutely. They must refer to some standard of values, and values, we know, are hopelessly subjective. We resent the arrogance implied in judgments which seem to have any tinge of absoluteness about them. . . . We have come to believe less and less in any absolute criteria." In *Criticism, History and Critical Relativism,* Mr. Brooks asked, "How is a critic, who is plainly the product of his own day and time, hopelessly entangled in the twentieth century, to judge the poems of his own day— much less the poems of the past—sub specie aeternitatis!"

True, the voice of Mr. Eliot was that of the practising poet, the craftsman for whom criticism was understandably a rationale for practice; while the voice of Mr. Brooks was that of the academician, the critic. But the real distinction between Eliot and Brooks lay in their understanding of the tradition. Eliot would have revived the unification of sensibility inherent in the Christian tradition, but somewhat dissipated since the early seventeenth century; whereas Brooks, sympathetic with that tradition, would have sought unification within each individual work of art, judging a poem "not by the truth or falsity, as such, of the idea which it incorporated, but rather by its character, its drama—by its coherence, sensitivity, depth, richness, and tough-mindedness."

Brooks was intent upon denying the "heresy of critical relativism" which would reduce literature to cultural history by putting a poem, as it were, in direct competition with historical, scientific, and philosophical propositions. Still, he did succeed in moving into a relativism which may not have been cultural, but which was nonetheless heretical. It was heresy, certainly, from Mr. Eliot's Christian perspective; and it was heresy, I would contend, from the perspective of twentieth-century values as they began emerging during the middle decades.

One may begin, like Brooks, with certain values against which the art may be tested: the resolution of tensions revealed by wit, paradox, irony; the insistence that art is organic, to be examined within its own individual framework, and dissociated from problems of truth, logic, science, and religion; the assumption that poetry is a mimetic process, representing a series of unique experiences which share common denominators, such as language, rhythm, imagery, etc. To a major extent, Brooks's structural analyses of poems were in direct line with the structural analyses that were becoming increasingly inherent in the study of the physical sciences, to psychology, history, sociology, anthropology, linguistics, grammar. To some extent, the method was implicit in a pure form even in painting and sculpture, in novels and poetry, and was beginning to invade the newest art, the cinema.

But ultimately, I must confess, there is a certain sterility about art which exists only as organic structure. There is a vacuousness about criticism as structural analysis, revealing only common tensions at work within independent organisms. There is indeed a certain knowledge to be derived from dissecting a bird—and a certain pleasure, as well. But birds are also to be caught, to be eaten, to be written about, to be heard, to be pursued "on the viewless wings of Poesy," or "set upon a golden bough to sing / To lords and ladies of Byzantium." Poems, like birds, are analyzable—but there is a lot more about poetry than its artistic structure, the architectonics of inner tensions, the skeletal frame of images, or the pattern of ironies.

Cleanth Brooks did share with the twentieth century—with John Crowe Ransom and Robert Penn Warren, Allen Tate, R. P. Blackmur and W. K. Wimsatt—a concentrated emphasis upon structuring. His original intent, to examine the poetic experience by analyzing the poem *qua* poem, successfully moved us away from rather peripheral concerns with the source of the poem, its author, its impression upon the reader, its historical affiliation. The movement was altogether necessary, and so successful that Eliot himself began cautioning about the direction that structural criticism was taking, and in 1956 he suggested in *The Frontiers of Criticism* that current critical standards were in need of readjustment. Earlier, in his second

essay on Milton, Eliot had been prepared to concede that poetic standards had changed; the seventeenth-century poet was no longer dangerous as a model. Now, he cautioned, undue emphasis upon the understanding can lure in the direction of science the critic who searches for mere explanation. Almost a half century ago, undue emphasis upon enjoyment threatened to entice the critic into the impressionistic and subjective, so that art became merely an amusing pastime. Now, Eliot urged in 1956, we have to be on our guard against the purely explanatory and descriptive.

Aside from this emphasis upon explanatory or descriptive criticism, Brooks revealed other characteristics, recognizable as modern or twentieth-century. He had an understanding of and sympathy for psychological time dimensions. He was suspicious of absolutes. He recognized the extent to which men tend to color reality by their own personality. He was aware of the extent to which we are entangled in our own age. Keats, of course, was trying to work his way through these very problems. So were most of the other leading nineteenth-century poets and critics and novelists. This is what makes them so very much within *the* tradition—within Leavis' notion of tradition, if not within Eliot's.

But Keats, like his contemporaries, demanded that art function with a social and moral base. He assumed that the writing of poetry demanded a world other than the poem and the self, a world filled with men and nightingales, gnats and urns, poetry and love. The creation of poetry and the creation of a soul were for Keats equally predicated upon an inter-action, an inter-relationship, and an inter-dependency of men. This was the basis for all values.

Because Mr. Brooks saw the critic "hopelessly entangled in the twentieth century," both poem and explication seemed to need existences independent of everything but one another. Brooksian analysis seemed to aim, not at disengaging the critic from the poem, but at disengaging him from all else other than the poem. And yet, if the critic is indeed "hopelessly entangled," it seems to me that analysis ought properly to reveal the way in which that entanglement "hopelessly" colors and distorts perception. Certainly the virtues of Freudian analysis

emerge neither from the unveiling of complexities nor from the uncovering of entanglements within the human personality—although it is complex and entangled enough!—but from the ultimate freedom through which we are enabled to master ourselves, to achieve through our mature and our reasoned state a creative rather than a destructive existence. This is, after all, the essence of *the* tradition inherited from the Greeks and the Bible, from Chaucer and Shakespeare, from Donne and Milton, Keats, Hopkins, Yeats, and from Eliot himself: the creative, humane, enlightened, and "examined life" which for Socrates was alone worth living. This is, after all, the essence of the truly liberated spirit which has always in the long tradition of Western culture been hostile to destructiveness, inhumanity, darkness, ignorance, and chaos.

# 14
# The Heresy of Egotism

From Plato's *Ion* to Keats's *Ode on a Grecian Urn,* the pursuit of beauty has taken many forms. Cleanth Brooks's *Well Wrought Urn* is one of many such pursuits, for literary criticism essays to tell us how beauty has been captured by the poet, so that we as readers may ourselves better capture the poem. Criticism can tell us this truly or falsely, beautifully or badly. Plato's *Ion,* for example, is not just a dialectic about the nature of beauty. It is also, and perhaps primarily, a beautiful dialectic—like Shelley's *Defence* and Sidney's *Apologie.*

Socrates' concern in the *Ion* is with Homer. Yet the discerning reader recognizes that the beauties of Homer are not to be confused with either the beauties of Plato or Plato's conception of Homeric beauty. Similarly, Keats's *Ode on a Grecian Urn* is not to be confused with what the critics have been saying, for almost a century and a half now, about the ode; or with what Keats himself had to say about the ode; or, indeed, with what we ourselves perceive in the ode: its patterns of imagery; its development of ideas and attitudes; its structure of rhythms and rhymes. The ode has one kind of existence. What is said about the ode has another kind of existence.

These two existences certainly share, or should share, some

common ground. But insofar as we confuse these two existences, insofar as the one is for us inextricably bound up with
the other, the critical act has failed. It has become imprisoning,
rather than emancipative, for instead of learning how to capture the poem, we are instead captured by it—or worse, held
captive by the criticism about the poem.

Eliot offers one interpretation of the critical act, as the grasp
of truths involved in a unified Christian tradition. Brooks offers
another, representing the organism of individual ironies and
paradoxes.

James Joyce suggests yet a third at the close of *Portrait*, when
Stephen holds forth about the many cultural distinctions involved in the pursuit of beauty by the Greek, the Turk, the
Chinese, the Copt, the Hottentot. In the earlier and expanded
version of *Stephen Hero*, the protagonist had enunciated with
greater clarity the way out of this cultural relativism, through a
scrutiny of the "apprehensive faculty":

No esthetic theory . . . is of any value which investigates with the aid of
the lantern of tradition. What we symbolise in black the Chinaman may
symbolise in yellow: each has his own tradition. Greek beauty laughs at
Coptic beauty and the American Indian derides them both. It is almost
impossible to reconcile all tradition whereas it is by no means impossible
to find the justification of every form of beauty which has been adored on
the earth by an examination into the mechanism of esthetic apprehension
whether it be dressed in red, white, yellow or black. We have no reason for
thinking that the Chinaman has a different system of digestion from that
which we have though our diets are quite dissimilar. The apprehensive
faculty must be scrutinized in action.

For Stephen, the scrutiny of the "apprehensive faculty" is a
problem at once psychological and aesthetic, like Conrad's concern with the supreme task of the novelist "by the power of the
written word to make you hear, to make you feel—it is before
all, to make you see." For both, perception is dependent upon
the perceiver.

Investigating without "the aid of the lantern of tradition,"
Stephen can produce art of some value. When the Greek comes
to recognize the extent to which home, country, or gods color
and distort his apprehensive faculty, his scrutiny of what a
thing is and what it is not, then—and only then—can he free

himself from his bondage, from the nets these would fling over him in capturing his soul. Only then can he achieve the "epiphanies" which must be the basis of art. When Stephen Dedalus comes to recognize the extent to which nationality, language, home, family, or religion blur the focus of his apprehensive faculty, confusing for him the nature of what is with what he would have them be, then true apprehension—and true art—becomes possible.

Mr. Brooks has suggested that values are "hopelessly subjective." The critic—and probably the poet, also—is "plainly the product of his own day and time, hopelessly entangled in the twentieth century." Because "we have no confidence in absolutes of any kind," the critic is seemingly driven into a restricted analysis of "the structure of the poem as an organism." And yet, if we are "hopelessly entangled," as Mr. Brooks suggests, then structural analysis scarcely represents a reliable appraisal of a poem or play or novel; it can only reflect the entanglement of a twentieth-century critic, and never the poem or play or novel itself. Enlightenment only through analysis would appear to be much of a delusion, insofar as analysis purports to tell us what is really going on within the poem. Without "confidence in absolutes," the structural analyst seems curiously to have absolute confidence in himself—in his own analyzing, critical, dissective powers.

Entanglements are indeed hopeless, unless we use our awareness as the first step toward real emancipation. Having recognized the extent to which our twentieth-century vision entangles us in a poem, we ought to begin recognizing the need for scrutinizing our apprehensive faculty, like Stephen Dedalus. We ought to be prepared to liberate ourselves from, rather than indulge ourselves in, the particular prejudices and irrational quirks which constitute this twentieth-century vision. If a poem is really an organism with its own right to existence, then the critic has no right to superimpose his own entangled existence upon the poem.

Like the poetic act, the critical act is essentially emancipative. The poet liberates himself from the imprisoning demands of the past, in order to facilitate his ultimate capture of beauty. The critic may stop short of the poetic process, but he emanci-

pates himself in much the same way, in order to select and reproduce from the mass before him. The history of literary criticism has told us alternately that poetry is knowledge; that poetry is power; that poetry is truth; that poetry is beauty; that poetry is tradition; that poetry is tension or irony or paradox. Poets themselves have been saying, rather implicitly, what Archibald MacLeish has said directly: that poetry simply is; it "should not mean / But be." I am not suggesting yet another way of looking upon poetry. I am suggesting, rather, another way of looking upon criticism. Poetry may indeed be; it may exist within its own right. But criticism has no such right—except possibly insofar as it is itself a work of art, in which case its beauty is more important than its truth. But a critic who would operate with true or valid criticism must distinguish between the being of a poem (its potentialities) and the being of the reader (his potentialities) .

Like most modern readers, Cleanth Brooks has argued, and most cogently, against the "heresy of paraphrase" which would offer a restatement of the work, as if in the distilled meaning is to be found the fulfillment of craft. Like MacLeish, Brooks has argued that "a true poem is a simulacrum of reality . . . by *being* an experience rather than any mere statement about experience or any mere abstraction from experience."

In Mr. Brooks's canon there are other kinds of heresy. There is what has been called "the heresy of biography" which would confuse the life with the art, confusing what Keats the man meant or was unconsciously driven to assert in the *Ode on a Grecian Urn* with what the poem itself is and does. To be driven back to an examination of Keats's conversations, his letters, his readings, his friends' letters to him and about him, the preoccupations of the age—all of which are available—seemingly would not provide Mr. Brooks with the organicism of the ode itself.

There are, of course, many other kinds of heresy. There is the heresy of history; the heresy of religion; the heresy of psychology; the heresy of Marxism; the heresy of source-hunting and footnotes and academic quibbling; the heresy of primal myth and archetypal patterns. These are all heresies, insofar as they offer a substitute for the art itself—neatly clipping Keats's ode,

say, to fit some historical concept, judging it relative to theological assumptions, subverting it for purposes of psychology, placing it in competition with socio-economic theories, testing it only against possible origins or parallels, smothering it with pedantry, identifying it with *Allerlei-Wissenschaft*. These are all, I suspect, heretical acts from Mr. Brooks's perspective—although they are equally heretical now from the perspective of most modern critics. Insofar as these approaches do not assert the primacy of pattern within the poem itself, they tend to subvert the wholism of art.

Unfortunately, critical procedure which offers only the analysis of a work of art now threatens to become the substitute for the art form it is dissecting. Increasingly, poetry has been dehumanized by critics, as it has been transformed into a structure, a pattern of images, an arrangement of symbols. Increasingly, the better poem is the more complex, the most susceptible to analysis. The more complex one discovers a poem to be, the better critic he is. It is no accident that this mid-twentieth century has been called "The Age of Criticism." A label more apt might have been "The Age of Non-Commitment," or perhaps "The Dissociated Era," for literary critics have dissociated themselves from the human values implicit in critical judgment. Cleverness, ingenuity, sensitivity, agility in the analyst seem increasingly to supercede, to take on an importance more primary than the art itself. When a fifty-line ode needs a fifty-page explication or merits a lengthy anthology of divergent analyses, then something dangerous is happening to our own critical standards. Something dangerous is happening to the inherent relationship between art and analysis, between beauty and our critical apperception of beauty. I have the feeling that somehow in the process the ode is being destroyed.

This is a heresy of the largest order, it seems to me. Having been diverted from other heresies by Mr. Brooks's very necessary and very well-meaning attempts, we seem to have fallen into a brook of another kind. Now, we seem to be drowning in it. Even Mr. Brooks has diverged somewhat from his earlier position. Keats himself would have labeled this "the heresy of the egotistical sublime."

It is relatively easy now—after the analysts, the explicators,

the old "new" critics—to avoid the biographical or the para-
phrastic heresy. Instead, we have begun confusing criticism
with poetry, ourselves with the poem. The "heresy of egotism,"
I would suggest, opens up the danger that through criticism we
shape the features of the ode from our own being, so that it
becomes through our entanglements with it little more than an
image of self. It turns into a mirror of our own facility, a
fictional form of our own ego. It is perhaps the greatest heresy
of all for the poem to offer only an excuse for the existence of
the critic. The heresy of egotism denies not only the poem's
right to existence, uncolored by the critic's entanglements; it
denies also the essential existence of the critic whose being must
be postulated only upon the act of exegesis and seemingly
upon nothing else. It is almost as if the contemporary critic
lacks the courage—or the wisdom—to be anything other than
an explicator or an analyst.

Impressionistic criticism, so familiar during the earliest decades of this century, was never really dangerous. It offered, for
what it was, a subjective and personal examination of works of
art. But structural analysis which pretends to objectivity is most
dangerous. It would exclude all approaches other than the
structural. It would admit to a poem only its artistic form. It
would deny the ordered attitudes and values which give that
form meaning, just as it would ignore the critic's own structure,
the form in which he himself is "hopelessly entangled" and
from which he derives his judgments. True, some art, like some
paintings of modern abstract expressionists, admits only structural arrangement, revealing only the architectonics of color,
line, and mass. But even then, it would seem, the critic's function is to point to the meaning and value of that design. Or its
meaninglessness. And its valuelessness.

The critical act, like the creative act, demands a liberation
from self, not an indulgence in self; an emancipation from the
shackles of self, not a turning loose of self. The self may be
pleasure-seeking, luxuriant, voluptuary; but it may also be
inquisitive, coldly intellectual, highly censorious. The one is no
more admirable than the other—in men, or in critics. T. S.
Eliot has suggested in *Tradition and the Individual Talent*
that "the poet has not a 'personality' to express, but a particu-

lar medium." Yet, worship at the altar of artistic form, it seems
to me, is no less abhorrent than worship at the altar of self.
Ultimately, it is just as destructive.

Mr. Brooks is quite right about the critic being "entangled"
in his own century. And he is quite right about a poem being
its own best context. And yet, if the critic is to fling himself
within the confines of a poem, he must learn how to extricate
himself. And he must know what it is that is both flung and
extricated. Eliot's famous analogy—the introduction of finely
filiated platinum into a chamber containing oxygen and sul-
phur dioxide—defined the process of depersonalization and its
relationship to tradition as analogous to that of the catalyst. In
its time, the analogy was fascinating. But I suspect that we have
come increasingly to see that depersonalization is not always
desirable, for poets or for critics. In its extreme, it can be the
basis for neutrality, disinvolvement, moral detachment. We
have come to see that there is a vast difference between a poet
and a catalyst, although the difference between a critic and a
catalyst is rapidly disappearing. Like Keats's chameleon poet,
the critic must draw from the poem whatever color he can. But
he ought to do this without the heresy of egotism. He ought to
avoid lending the poem his own color—or his lack of color. A
poem should be its own best context. But a poem that exists
wholly within its own context is a very sterile poem indeed.

John Keats, as man, no longer exists. And the age in which
he lived no longer exists either. Whatever it is that he was, he
exists now only in his works. Keats as man—to paraphrase
Sartre—is now nothing more than a little phosphate and cal-
cium carbonate with salts and water. A Keatsian ode, however,
is a very real and very existent thing. Any information we
might garner about Keats the man is significant, but only insofar as it can tell us about the presently existent poem. This is
the value, the enormous value, of Keats's letters. They tell us
about the poetry-making process, about those values inherent
within the odes. This is the value of Haydon's journals and
Woodhouse's scrapbook, and of the hundreds of letters written
by his friends to and about Keats. And this is, after all, the
value of the wealth of research and criticism and scholarship
done on Keats. They reveal to us varied means of distinguish-

ing Keats's attitudes as reflected in the odes and, say, Haydon's perception of the poet; or our own perception; or Keats's perception of himself. In the final analysis, the whole of history—the entirety of Western culture—might lend itself to the reading of a Keatsian ode. We should not be satisfied with less. This is the only context in which any poem can properly be viewed. It may as art exist within its own context; but the context is considerably larger than a pattern of ironies or images or paradoxes.

The critic's task is a formidable one. Perhaps it is even an impossible one. He must demand from a poem its largest context, the whole of Western culture up to Keats. He must demand from himself yet a larger context, whatever has gone into his own making, the whole of Western culture up to himself. It is reclamation work, and not unlike Freud's vision of psychotherapy as a draining of the Zuyder Zee. It demands a knowledge of what is and has been, for Keats and for one's self; but also it demands a recognition of the potentialities of the future—for us, and for the poem itself.

I am not suggesting that poetry be approached with yet another kind of heresy, the "heresy of historicism," which would subordinate the art to that which is already past and shackle the critic as an amanuensis of time. History lies within us and within art. The true meaning of the past is its ever-presence. It does not lie behind us as background or above us as an inviolable master. To free himself from the demands of history, the critic—like the poet—must perform the emancipative act, recognizing the heresy of egotism, the extent to which self casts its own shadow.

# Acknowledgments

Throughout, I have relied upon H. W. Garrod's edition of *The Poetical Works of John Keats* (Oxford, 1958), with permission of Clarendon Press, Oxford; and upon Hyder Edward Rollins' superb editions of *The Letters of John Keats* (Cambridge, Mass., 1958) and *The Keats Circle* (Cambridge, Mass., 1948), with permission of Harvard University Press. Quotations from letters to and from Keats, from Woodhouse's scrapbook, and from Keats's poetry, are from these editions—although I deviate slightly from Rollins' faithful rendering of the text; whenever general comprehension might be enhanced, Keats's erratic spelling and punctuation have been modified slightly.

Translation from Virgil's *Eclogue* is by Frank Justus Miller; from Sophocles' *Antigone*, by F. Storr; from Plato's *Ion*, by W. R. M. Lamb; from Aeschylus' *Prometheus*, by Herbert Weir Smyth. All are reprinted by permission of Harvard University Press and The Loeb Classical Library.

The frontispiece, Haydon's sketch of John Keats, appears through the courtesy of The National Portrait Gallery in London. Nicolas Poussin's *Selene and Endymion* is from the collection of The Detroit Institute of Arts and appears with their permission. *Endymion and the Moon,* Gian Battista Cima's painting as photographed by Luigi Vaghi, is from The National Gallery at Parma. *Endymion and Selene* by Michel François André-Bardon is from the collection

of The California Palace of the Legion of Honor. Peter Paul Rubens' painting of *Diana and Endymion* appears through the courtesy of the Trustees of The National Gallery in London. *Endymion Sleeping* by Anne-Louis Girodet is from The Louvre, while the sarcophagus of *Diana and Endymion* is from the collection of The Capitoline Museum in Rome. The plaque, *Diana Visiting Endymion,* appears through the kindness of The Wedgwood Museum in Barlaston, Stoke-on-Trent, England. The two photographs from the Elgin Marbles—the heifer, and the gods and heroes—are by courtesy of the Trustees of The British Museum in London.

Brief acknowledgment is all too inadequate for David Battle who struggled with problems of designing this book, and for the various friends and colleagues who have read and commented judiciously on parts of the text during various phases of its development.

Excerpts from the corrected 1964 edition of James Joyce's *A Portrait of the Artist as a Young Man* are by permission of The Viking Press. Permission to quote from Cleanth Brooks's *The Well Wrought Urn* and from T. S. Eliot's *Selected Essays* has been kindly granted by Harcourt, Brace & World, Inc.

Parts of this volume have appeared, although in a somewhat different form, in other publications. Some of Chapter 1 appeared originally in *Apollo, The Magazine of the Arts,* LXXXIII, No. 45, for November 1965. A section of Chapter 6 appeared in *The Explicator,* XV (1957) as "Keats' *Endymion,* I, 1–35," and another in *Modern Language Quarterly,* XVIII, No. 2 (1957) as "The 'Fears' of John Keats."

My critical obligations are too multiple and too apparent for anyone acquainted with the scholarship on Keats. I have learned much from Sidney Colvin's short study, a book singularly refreshing still, despite its age. And I am much obligated to Walter Jackson Bate's several books; to chapters from David Perkins and D. G. James; to Lionel Trilling's penetrating essays; and in particular to the incredible thoroughness of Earl R. Wasserman's detailed analyses.

Throughout, I have tried not so much to distinguish between my newer insights and the older borrowed insights, as to present a fairly coherent picture of the artistic process at work with Keats. Thus, although I distinguish sharply between Keats's use of the sympathetic imagination and the functioning of the negative capability, a distinction somewhat diffused in Bate's studies, I see no reason to quarrel here with Bate's understanding when he opens up so much more than he obscures. In much the same way, Wasserman's emphasis upon a spatial movement in Keats, outside of

earthly dimensions at "heaven's bourn," is countered here by a stress upon a temporal movement within the confines of mortality and without supernatural overtones. I hesitate to wrest out of their context some of my less orthodox observations about the poet: the advantage of looking upon Keats as yet another variant of classicism; the importance of the "vale of Soul-making" letter, so crucial to Keats's non-conventional way of looking upon immortality; the distinction between things and values, and the poet's emphasis upon an intensity of pursuit, rather than teleological goals; his concern with inner time dimensions, and his struggle to coordinate the existential present with chronometric time units. There is too much to be lost, I suspect, by stressing these newer perspectives at the expense of the old, thrusting my own critical view into the foreground at the expense of Keats and of the huge and invaluable work done during the past half-century and more by students of Keats. If this small volume has been able to shed new light on Keats, this is because of my obligations, not despite them.

# Index